The Art of Loving

The Art of Loving

Female Subjectivity and Male
Discursive Traditions
in Shakespeare's Tragedies

Evelyn Gajowski

DELAWARE

Newark: University of Delaware Press
London and Toronto: Associated University Presses

Associated University Presses
440 Forsgate Drive
Cranbury, NJ 08512

Associated University Presses
25 Sicilian Avenue
London WC1A 2QH, England

Associated University Presses
P.O. Box 39, Clarkson Pstl. Stn.
Mississauga, Ontario,
L5J 3X9 Canada

The paper used in this publication meets the requirements of the American National Standard for Permanence of Paper for Printed Library Materials Z39.48-1984.

Library of Congress Cataloging-in-Publication Data

Gajowski, Evelyn.
 The art of loving : female subjectivity and male discursive
traditions in Shakespeare's tragedies / Evelyn Gajowski.
  p. cm.
 Includes bibliographical references and index.
 ISBN 0-87413-398-X (alk. paper)
 1. Shakespeare, William, 1564–1616—Tragedies. 2. Shakespeare,
William, 1564–1616—Knowledge—Psychology. 3. Shakespeare, William,
1564–1616—Characters—Women. 4. Sex differences (Psychology) in
literature. 5. Femininity (Psychology) in literature.
6. Subjectivity in literature. 7. Women in literature. 8. Love in
literature. 9. Tragedy. I. Title.
PR2983.G35 1992
822.3'3—dc20   90-50430
                                                              CIP

PRINTED IN THE UNITED STATES OF AMERICA

To Harvey

Contents

. . . this we were, this is how we tried to love,
and these are the forces they had ranged against us,
and these are the forces we had ranged within us,
within us and against us, against us and within us.
　　　　　—Adrienne Rich, "Twenty-One Love Poems,"
　　　　　　The Dream of a Common Language

Acknowledgments

When a work such as this—conceived, written, and revised over several years—finally reaches publication, one is in the position of carrying on a dialogue with a multitude of critics and theorists as well as several of one's own prior selves. The list of intellectual and personal debts grows long indeed.

I would like to thank the members of the reference staffs of the Folger Shakespeare Library, the Stanford University Libraries, and the McHenry Library at the University of California, Santa Cruz, for their kind assistance.

My work on heterosexual relations in Shakespeare's texts was encouraged by the work of feminist Shakespeareans, particularly Coppélia Kahn, Carol Thomas Neely, and Marianne Novy.

More recently, I have been encouraged by the work of women in related fields: philosopher Martha Nussbaum and psychoanalysts Nancy Chodorow, Dorothy Dinnerstein, Jane Flax, Carol Gilligan, and Jean Baker Miller on the relational aspects of the human animal under patriarchy and the work on subjectivity—particularly female subjectivity—by feminist theorists such as Teresa deLauretis, bell hooks, Elizabeth Fox-Genovese, and Adrienne Rich, among others, who eloquently contest elitist assumptions about the death of the author and the death of the subject at a juncture when women, ethnic minorities, and working-class people are, for the first time under patriarchy, occupying subject and author positions in substantial numbers.

For reading and responding to an earlier version of this work in its entirety, I am grateful to Deborah Ellis, Robert Ornstein, P. K. Saha, and Walter Strauss. Among the community of Shakespeareans from whose responses parts of this work have benefited are Susan Baker, Kent Cartwright, Lars Engle, Coppélia Kahn, Dorothea Kehler, David McCandless, Thomas Moisan, Frank Morral, Joseph Pequigney, Phyllis Rackin, Deborah Robinson, Kay Stanton, and Virginia Vaughan.

A section of chapter 3 was previously published under the title "The Female Perspective in *Othello*" in Othello: *New Perspectives*

(Fairleigh Dickinson University Press, 1990).

For lengthy discussions of several of the issues herein, for encouragement during more than one crisis, and for the shared conviction that Shakespeare is not a patriarchal bard, I am indebted to Kay Stanton.

I have benefited over the years from exchanges with students and colleagues at several universities. Among those I would like to single out at the University of California, Santa Cruz (when the book was in its final stages of publication), are the students in my senior seminar, Studies in Shakespeare, during the spring of 1989, who, when subjected to the ideas herein, entertained them with a mixture of skepticism and generosity, intelligence and humor. An uncommon pedagogical experience for teacher and student alike, that seminar ranks among my fondest memories. And for many kindnesses, great and small, I am deeply grateful to Michael Warren.

I am indebted to Jay Halio, Chair of the Editorial Board at the University of Delaware Press, for his interest in the manuscript in its earliest incarnation and for his kindness at several junctures throughout the publication process.

I feel privileged to have studied Shakespeare with Robert Ornstein; my teaching and writing continue to be inspired by his humane model. I am particularly thankful to him for tossing off the comment in graduate lecture that women in Shakespeare are more mature in love than men—the seed that planted this book in my brain.

Finally, the dedication of this book to my husband, Harvey Berenberg, is a token of my appreciation for the precious gifts of time and space in which to write.

The Art of Loving

1

Intersections of Genre and Gender in Shakespeare's Love Tragedies

> But what if the object started to speak?
> —Luce Irigaray, *Speculum of the Other Woman*

A human being walks a tightrope, Jacob Bronowski remarks, between the acknowledgment of social responsibility, on the one hand, and the desire to fulfill individual wishes, on the other. No other animal faces this particular dilemma. Other species are either social or solitary; the human species alone aspires, as Bronowski puts it, "to be both in one, a social solitary" (1973, 411). The genres of comedy and tragedy represent this unique duality of the human condition—the balancing act between responsibility and individual desire, the divided aspiration in the human psyche toward the social and the solitary. Comedy represents human beings primarily as social creatures; it celebrates human commonality by emphasizing the cohesiveness of members of a given community. Tragedy represents human beings primarily as solitary creatures; it celebrates human uniqueness by emphasizing the isolation of an individual from the social milieux.[1]

Love tragedies, because they emphasize the relatedness or connectedness of two extraordinary individuals isolated from ordinary worlds, are located at the intersection of comedy and tragedy. More so than either comedy or tragedy, they interrogate the divided human aspiration toward the social and the solitary, the attempt "to be both in one." In their concern with the individual's striving for relatedness or connectedness, they differ from nonromantic tragedies. They represent human beings not simply as autonomous individuals with the power to assert personal values in the face of a hostile universe but, as Leonora Leet Brodwin notes, as relational individuals with the power to create a sphere of emotional intimacy in that hostile universe (1971, 6).[2]

Within the dramatic worlds of Shakespeare's romantic comedies, the characteristic psychosocial pattern is that of a movement away from the isolated individual toward relationship or connection. Susan Snyder emphasizes this psychosocial pattern when she describes the movement in the comedies as "some form of *I* become *we*" (1985). Shakespeare's love tragedies uniquely retain this comic pattern of the love story, but transform it by enclosing it in a larger tragic action. This pattern accounts for the comic quality of the first two acts of *Romeo and Juliet* and *Othello*—neither play is as dark as *Hamlet*, *King Lear*, and *Macbeth* are from the outset. It accounts as well for the lightness and humor that characterize Cleopatra's Alexandrian scenes and the sense of triumph that dominates the final moments of *Antony and Cleopatra*.

It is a critical commonplace that Shakespeare's comedies inevitably conclude in the celebration of social harmony as symbolized by the wedding ceremony. Critics further observe that the examination of the state of marriage in *Othello* takes up where the comedies leave off. Indeed, when we consider all three love tragedies—*Romeo and Juliet*, *Othello*, *Antony and Cleopatra*—in chronological order, we notice a shift of emphasis from courtship and nuptials to the drama of a marriage or an enduring relationship. The action of the first two acts of *Romeo and Juliet* follows most closely the pattern of the comedies. Because the lovers meet at the end of act 1 and marry at the end of act 2, the emphasis falls on courtship as well as marriage. In *Othello*, the lovers' meeting, courtship, and elopement are donnés of the dramatic action although the drama of the first two acts depicts a romantic love comparable to that depicted in *Romeo and Juliet* and the comedies. *Antony and Cleopatra* deals with a heterosexual relationship that has endured many years yet, as in *Romeo and Juliet* and *Othello*, Shakespeare focuses on the problems of mutual realization of self and other, or what I shall call *intersubjectivity*.

Whereas in the comedies the lovers often are members of the same social group, the love tragedies emphasize the obstacles the lovers must overcome by exacerbating the social differences between them: a Capulet chooses a Montague, a Venetian chooses a Moor, an Egyptian queen chooses a Roman triumvir. Too, the social and political contexts within which the love relationships are set have greater consequences than the wars the male protagonists return from in *Much Ado* or set off on in *All's Well*. Military action and ideals of honor are brought to bear upon the love story either directly, as in *Romeo and Juliet* and *Antony and Cleopatra*, or indirectly as in *Othello*. The principal way Shakespeare opens up love (the traditional subject matter of comedy) for tragic treatment is by exploring its psychological implications.

For all the similarities which critics note between *The Comedy of Errors* and the New Comedy of ancient Rome, there are significant differences. As early as his first attempt at comedy, Shakespeare emphasizes the expression of feeling. The distinction between *The Comedy of Errors* and the comedies of Plautus and Terence lies not in the device of discovery, as Madeleine Doran reminds us, but in the poetic expression of feeling upon the occasion of that discovery. Sentiment is minimal or absent from Plautus's and Terence's treatment of heterosexual relations; the discovery of the romantic background of male or female protagonist is, as she puts it, "merely a convenient device to untie the knot of complications" ([1954] 1964, 172–73). In the love tragedies the sense of resolution depends even less than in the comedies on plot device and even more on the possibility of transformation by means of a deepening of consciousness. What Edward Quinn says of *King Lear* is also true of the love tragedies: self-knowledge is achieved through indirect means—through learning how to love (1985, xxiii–xxiv). Indeed, Shakespeare sharpens the focus on love as not only a communion of consciousness but as a way of creating awareness in another. As two people with two different states of psychological organization and desires interact, the outcome is the creation of a new state in each person, as psychoanalyst Jean Baker Miller points out. Both people change as a result of the interaction, but in different ways and at different rates ([1976] 1986, 128–29).

Because the emphasis in the love tragedies is on the psychological as well as the social, the obstacles to the love relationship are more complicated than the "blocking characters" that are one of the essential ingredients of comedy for Northrop Frye ([1957] 1970, 165). Vestiges of this force remain to be sure. The Capulet-Montague feud and Brabantio's opposition to Desdemona's and Othello's marriage remind us of Egeus's opposition to Hermia and Lysander in *A Midsummer Night's Dream*. Capulet's command that Juliet marry Paris—an arranged marriage become an enforced marriage—reminds us of Egeus's command that Hermia marry Demetrius and Portia's subjection, literally and metaphorically, to her father's will in *The Merchant of Venice*. Paternal opposition is merely one manifestation, though, of Shakespeare's continuing interest in the tragedies as well as the comedies in the disparity between male and female attitudes toward love, sex, and marriage.

The line of romantic males extends from *The Comedy of Errors* through the romances: Antipholus of Syracuse, Lucentio, Proteus, Romeo, Paris, Lysander, Bassanio, Claudio, Orlando, Orsino, Troilus, Cassio, Antony, Posthumus, Ferdinand. The strand of anti-romantic males is equally evident: Antipholus of Ephesus, Petruchio,

Valentine, Mercutio, Berowne, Benedick, Bertram, Iago, Octavius, Iachimo, Leontes. Such groupings blur rather than sharpen lines of individual characterization, of course, yet underlying these two different masculine[3] responses to love, sex, and women we discern the influence of medieval and classical literature. Indeed, romantic and antiromantic discursive practices[4] differentiate the two main varieties of early modern English comedy—the romantic comedy of Lyly, Peele, Dekker, and Shakespeare and the social comedy of Jonson, Middleton, and others. The emphasis is on two different sets of human motives: "poetic longings for love and adventure," as Doran puts it, such as we find in any comedy by Shakespeare, and the "grosser appetites for women, money, or power," in comedies such as Jonson's *Volpone* and *The Alchemist*. The defining difference is one of tone: sympathetically expressed lyrical sentiment differentiates romantic comedy from the biting critical satire of social, didactic comedy ([1954] 1964, 149).

The antiromantic, or Ovidian, discursive tradition echoes down through the centuries from Ovid's *Ars Amatoria,* Andreas de Capellanus, and Jean de Meun through *gauloiserie* and fabliaux to Chaucer, Malory, Boccaccio, and the vituperative element of the sonnet sequences. The romantic, or Petrarchan, discursive tradition echoes from the Provençal troubadours, Chrétien, and Guillaume de Lorris through Dante and Petrarch to the blazon of the Elizabethan sonnet sequences. The pre-Shakespearean "juxtology"[5] of the two traditions originates in twelfth-century Provençal France with the origin of romantic love as a structure of thought in the western tradition. The personal nature of romantic love—as a relationship between two individuals—distinguishes it from the impersonal nature of both classical *eros,* or sexual desire, and Christian *agape,* or spiritual love, wherein the individuality of the female object of desire or love is of little consequence to the male producer of the text.

The most radical implication of the new belief, *amour courtois,* as Joseph Boone notes, is that the female sex, after centuries of denigration as man's inferior, the cause of his fall, and a lascivious creature of the flesh, is viewed as worthy of man's profound love. Desire on the part of the male rather than consummation becomes a literary end in itself (1987, 34–35). The two parts of *Roman de la Rose,* authored by Guillaume and Jean, embody side by side in one work the two masculine discursive practices. Dante's and Petrarch's idealizing of Beatrice and Laura are the progeny of Guillaume. The "curiously exacerbated misogyny, naturalism, and man's reduction to sex" of *gauloiserie* and fabliaux are, as Denis de Rougemont puts it, the progeny of Jean ([1940] 1983, 176). While some medievalists view

Roman de la Rose as a turning point from reverence to ridicule, its divided attitudes may be viewed within a larger historical pattern of alternating idealism and cynicism. Although the emphasis in Jean is on the negative, as C. S. Lewis points out, he is perpetuating tradition rather than initiating a cynical age ([1936] 1958, 145).

It is tempting to view *l'esprit gaulois* as opposed to the conventions of courtly love, the natural as opposed to the artificial, the animal as opposed to the spiritual, the secular as opposed to the religious. The glorification of sexuality, however, as Johan Huizinga maintains, performs as much of an idealizing, escapist function as does the glorification of chastity:

> The whole genre [*Les Cent Nouvelles Nouvelles* and the loose song] with its wilful neglect of all the natural and social complications of love, with its indulgence towards the lies and egotism of sexual life, and its vision of a never-ending lust, implies, no less than the screwed-up system of courtly love, an attempt to substitute for reality the dream of a happier life. It is once more the aspiration towards the life sublime, but this time viewed from the animal side. It is an ideal all the same, even though it be that of unchastity. (1924, 99)

Masculine idealism and cynicism about women are, as Lewis puts it, "twin fruits on the same branch"; Petrarchan and Ovidian discursive practices are but "positive and negative poles of a single thing" ([1936] 1958, 145). No real contradiction exists between a cynical attitude and tragic romanticism, de Rougemont claims, because both *gauloiserie* and passion are escapes from the complex psychological reality of love. The sensuous, pornographic style of the fabliaux betrays an absence of realism that is identical to that of the idealizing courtly epics ([1940] 1983, 307, 186). Insofar as both discursive traditions constitute fictional escapes from the vulnerable psychological reality of love, the literary progeny of *Roman de la Rose* are not disparate but similar practices. Both mock marriage—Ovidian discourse mocks it "from below"; Petrarchan discourse mocks it "from above" (de Rougemont [1940] 1983, 187). Both objectify women—Ovidian discourse objectifies women by denigrating them; Petrarchan discourse objectifies women by idealizing them.[6]

Although lust, love, and marriage inhabit mutually exclusive conceptual universes for centuries, a literary ideal of romantic marriage emerges in early modern England (Boone 1987, 31–64; Dusinberre 1975). This Puritan phenomenon—a synthesis of love and marriage—is manifest, of course, as a powerful force in Shakespeare's dramatic worlds. It is nearly always framed, however, by both Ovidian and

Petrarchan discursive practices, which find expression as essential components of male camaraderie. The principle threat to romantic love and marriage, as throughout the courtly tradition, is honor; the ultimate sacrifice of a noble heart, as throughout the courtly tradition, is that of honor to love. Shakespeare's comedies—particularly *Two Gentlemen of Verona, Love's Labor's Lost, The Merchant of Venice,* and *Much Ado About Nothing*—reveal an increasing tension, when considered chronologically, between male friendship and heterosexual love.[7]

In the love tragedies male friendship and its attendant attitudes toward females take on a progressively greater destructive potential in opposition to heterosexual relationships. The multiple possibilities of comedy are replaced by the limited options of tragedy. While the comic world is one of "both/and," to quote Linda Bamber, the tragic world of is one of "either/or" (1982, 112). Whereas both homosocial and heterosexual bonding may occur in comedy, tragedy demands a choice on the part of the male protagonist between the two. In *Romeo and Juliet,* Mercutio's casualness and flippancy about sexuality and love, like that of the antiromantics of the comedies, are, perhaps, defenses against the threat of unhappy love; they serve, moreover, as foils to Romeo's romanticism. In *Othello,* however, the antiromantic discursive tradition culminates in the misogyny of Iago; it is a potent, lethal force in the dramatic world of that tragedy—one that has the power to erode Othello's nobility and cause Desdemona's death. And in *Antony and Cleopatra,* the misogyny that is epitomized by Philo and Octavius and the discursive practice of Orientalism conflate,[8] constituting the Roman ideology that dominates the entire known western world.

George Eliot remarks that Shakespeare's females "almost always *make love,* in opposition to the conventional notion of what is fitting for woman" (quoted in Dusinberre 1975, 72). Shakespeare, as Leah Marcus reminds us, is not necessarily a window into his contemporary dramatists (1989). Indeed, having inherited the Petrarchan and Ovidian discursive practices that frame the standard female object, he preeminently among his contemporaries disrupts these traditions, representing a radically new construction of romantic love and marriage. His texts subvert the traditional love triangle—female object framed by male idolators and cynics—when he transforms object into subject, activating her, and giving her voice.

The treatment of love in Roman comedy is most often "simply an infatuation or an urgency of possession," as Doran emphasizes, presented from the male point of view. The female character, if a virtuous one, is "wholly passive" and "rarely appears" ([1954] 1964, 173). The courtly lover ultimately desires union with a religious absolute, Brod-win notes. He achieves this union through purifying service to a lady who represents this absolute in apprehensible form (1971, 6). The secular idolatry of the lady on the pedestal in the later permutations of the courtly tradition is analogous to the religious worship of the Virgin in the dominant ideology of the medieval period, Roman Catholicism.[9] The process of the lover's ennoblement demands that he overcome a series of obstacles or pass a series of arduous trials. He is most often active, and the lady passive, throughout this process. The legacy of male description in praise of female beauty is, as Nancy Vickers puts it, "a legacy shaped predominantly by the male imagination for the male imagination." The blazon tradition is "the product of men talking to men about women" (1985, 96).

Neither the cruel, coy fair of the sonnet cycles nor the silent, passive maiden of medieval romance and Roman comedy, Shake-speare's female protagonists are instead articulate, active partners in love. And "to speak," as Catherine Belsey reminds us, "is to become a subject" (1988).[10] Shakespeare's females not only take the initiative in love but also express skepticism at the attitudinizing of the male protagonists. Language, like action, therefore, no longer falls ex-clusively within the male purview; eloquence no longer is merely a weapon in the assault upon female chastity. More so than his fellow playwrights Shakespeare is concerned, Dusinberre notes, "to dissolve artificial distinctions between the sexes." His females poke fun at masculine discursive practices: whether adored or despised, they comment on men's idolatry from the margins in the same way that his rustics and artisans comment on the court (1975, 153). As early as the sonnets and *Love's Labor's Lost*, Shakespeare satirizes Petrarchan conventions—"My mistress' eyes are nothing like the sun"—and holds up Berowne's and Navarre's "taffeta phrases" to the mockery of Rosaline and the Princess of France.[11] In the mature romantic come-dies, Beatrice's "Kill Claudio" shocks because it takes at face value Benedick's romantic offer, "Come, bid me do any thing for thee" (*Much Ado*, 4.1.288). Rosalind performs literary criticism of Or-lando's poetry. Olivia parodies the sonnet convention of anatomizing female beauty: "I will give out divers schedules of my beauty. It shall be inventoried, and every particle and utensil labell'd to my will: as, *item*, two lips, indifferent red; *item*, two grey eyes, with lids to them; *item*, one neck, one chin, and so forth" (*Twelfth Night*, 1.5.244–49).[12]

In a recent study of *Measure for Measure*, Marcia Riefer concludes that the world of comedy and the world of patriarchy are, if not mutually exclusive, incompatible and antithetical. The powerlessness of the Shakespearean female is a variable, she maintains, in a drama-turgical formula in which "the pervasiveness of chauvinism" and "the possibility of comic resolution" are indirectly proportional (1984, 169). The stronger the forces of patriarchy operating in a particular dramatic world, in other words, the less likely are the chances for comic resolution. Gender is connected to genre in complicated ways in Shakespeare's texts, as Riefer and other feminist critics point out. In genre after genre, the human impulses of love and power are time and again brought into conflict with one another. Baldly put, in Shakespeare's histories the impulse to power prevails; in Shake-speare's comedies the impulse to love prevails. Shakespeare heightens the conflict between these impulses in the tragedies, and nowhere more so than in the love tragedies where mixed generic elements jostle for primacy in a way that defies traditional generic categoriza-tion. Things are far more complex than such a simplistic scheme would suggest, of course, yet it is in the love tragedies that the empowered female protagonists of the comedies interpenetrate the tragic genre and even destabilize it.

The empowered female characters of the comedies are rightly cele-brated by "compensatory" feminist critics; the disempowered—even victimized—female characters of the tragedies are rightly noted by "justificatory" feminist critics.[13] To view the marriages of the comic females as nothing more than submissions to patriarchy, however, is to ignore the crucial significance in Shakespeare's texts of emotional bonds and intimate relationships—of relational, affiliative capacities of human beings of both sexes.[14] Accordingly, to view the deaths of the tragic females as victimizations by patriarchy—and no more than that—is to ignore the commentary that Shakespeare's texts make upon masculine impulses of possession, politics, and power.[15] Femi-nist critics recognize the significance of sexuality and love. Recent materialist/historicist studies, however—as Mary Beth Rose points out—consider representations of sexuality and love significant only insofar as they are relevant to "the manipulations of Elizabethan and Jacobean political power" and "mechanisms of economic exchange" (1988, 11).

The privileging of politics and power on the part of materialist/ historicist approaches in this way constitutes, I believe, a perpetua-tion and reinforcement of patriarchy. It has the effect, as Neely contends, of "putting woman in her customary place." Women con-tinue "to be marginalized, erased, displaced, allegorized"; their lan-guage and silence continue "to serve the newly dominant ideology" (1988, 7). It is damaging, moreover, to a genuinely feminist discourse because it deprivileges relationships between human beings, denying the power that relationships play in cultures and in texts. It is the difference between insisting, Creon-like, that families are subservient to the state and comprehending the far more complex psychosocial reality, that the state *is constituted of* families. To assume that political power is "more real—more worthy of analysis—" than sexual love and marriage is to overlook the interpenetrating relationship of the human impulses of power and love. It is, as Rose puts it, to ignore the "mixed, complex, and overlapping nature of public and private experience" (1988, 11).

As the Renaissance conception of the *self* rises in prominence, literary representations of marriage begin to assume a new symbolic role, "signifying the apex of the protagonist's growth and acquisition of an adult sense of identity" (Boone 1987, 48). In Shakespeare's love tragedies as in the comedies, self-realization occurs obliquely through learning how to love. The female protagonists are catalysts in this process of reconstructing male identity;[16] that is to say, they play a large part in bringing about change in the male protagonists without themselves undergoing a like fundamental change. The emphasis falls on their ability and their potential to teach the male protagonists in relational, rather than autonomous, ways of knowing. Juliet tutors Romeo in love, allowing him to surpass the roles of chivalric lover and chivalric avenger and making possible his metamorphosis from stereotypical Petrarchan lover to true lover. She draws him away from extrinsic concerns—the masculine blazon tradition, the feud, and male honor—toward an authentic emotional commitment grounded in faith in himself and in her. The emphasis on active generosity is made explicit in her quintessential expression of her love: "My bounty is as boundless as the sea, / My love as deep; the more I give to thee, / The more I have, for both are infinite" (*Romeo and Juliet*, 2.2.133–35). Juliet's characteristic generosity, confidence, and intimacy of expression make her the standard by which we gauge Romeo's development. What matters is that he reach her plane, wedding words to actions and emotions rather than speaking in clichés, lest we feel that she lives and dies a tragic protagonist while he is a nice boy tossed about by circumstance.

Desdemona's language, like Juliet's, is more direct and less rhetorical than her husband's; her candor, like Juliet's, conveys a more realistic, less romantic concept of love than his, as Rosalie Colie notes (1974, 167). She has, however, no effect upon him akin to that of Juliet upon Romeo. Rather than achieving self-realization, Othello discovers merely the simple truth of her innocence. Although he finally comes to understand the purity of her love, he fails to make the essential discovery that he is worthy of it. His confidence, natural in a general accustomed to a lifetime of commanding soldiers, would appear to sustain him in the new experience of love. One who has spent his life alone, however, scarcely can believe a love as rare as hers exists; thus he expresses "wonder" at their moment of greatest felicity, their greeting at Cyprus. Her love to him is at once precious and precarious; to experience the happiness of love is to experience the fear of its loss. The link between love and faith is even more crucial in this relationship than in that of Romeo and Juliet: "My life upon her faith!" (*Othello*, 1.3.294). Because love depends not only upon confidence in oneself but faith in another, Othello is vulnerable to Iago; his sense of wonder at Desdemona's love gives way to loss of faith.

In imagining Cleopatra not as the grand courtesan of all time but as devoted to Antony, Shakespeare breaks literary tradition (Bullough 1964, 218–38). She shares with Desdemona and Juliet a depth and totality of emotional commitment toward her lover and a comprehensive concept of love that includes but is not confined to the sexual. Unlike Desdemona and like Juliet she tutors her "husband" in love, enabling Antony to change from a soldier who views her as his "pleasure" to a lover reconciled at last with the knowledge that she is all he he desires in life. Her irony punctures Antony's romantic hyperboles, yet her poetic artistry immortalizes him: "His legs bestrid the ocean; his rear'd arm / Crested the world; his voice was propertied / As all the tuned spheres" (*Antony and Cleopatra*, 5.2.81–83). Her totality of being, moreover, her "infinite variety"— though it is repeatedly imaged merely as the ability to defy Roman appetite—in truth defies both Roman fascination with and revulsion of her. Not Egyptian but Roman "fetters" bind Antony: as in *Othello*, heroic language conveys an honorable past, a yet uncorrupted Rome whose disparity with the present haunts him. His sensitivity to the difference between his age and Octavius's youth internalizes this disparity between past and present and reveals his suspicion that he is irrelevant in Octavius's new order. His vacillation between insecurity and confidence in love parallels his alternating military defeat and victory in the political action. If Romeo's and Juliet's certainty in love—their unquestioning assumption of its value—imbues their love with purity, then Antony's uncertainty in love—his constant questioning of its value—imbues his and Cleopatra's love with impurity. Yet if "to be once in doubt" is so intolerable for Othello that he must "prove" doubt to be true, then repeated misunderstandings characterize Antony's and Cleopatra's love, as does their capacity for repeated reconciliation.

In Shakespeare's comedies, we are struck by the female protagonists' movement—or the illusion of their movement, through their unconventionality and the power of their language—into the realm of action. They escape the restrictions of the stereotypically feminine role and enjoy remarkable freedom through disguise, autonomy, and wit. Conversely, in Shakespeare's love tragedies, we are struck by the male protagonists' movement into the realm of emotional experience. They leave behind them the traditional arena of tragedy, the realm of action epitomizd by street fighting or the battlefield, and enter into a world for which they are unprepared. What A. D. Nuttall observes in relation to *Othello* is also true, metaphorically speaking, of each of the love tragedies: it is "the story of a hero who went into a house" (1983, 134). For the Jacobean tragedians, the emphasis falls on female protagonists who, as Robert Ornstein puts it, are excluded from "the worlds of action in which men may realize their potentialities." They are, perhaps, "more absorbed in and dependent upon emotional relationships: their fulfillment must lie in love and in marriage" ([1960] 1965, 172). For Shakespeare, though, in the love tragedies as in the comedies, the emphasis falls on female protagonists who are profounder in feeling, more realistic, and more mature in love than are the male protagonists. We know of love in Shakespeare, indeed, as something women feel for men. Regardless of whether or not his female protagonists are confined to or grounded in the private realm of personal relationships, they remain constant in the depth and totality of their emotional commitment. Absorbed instead with public concerns, with ideals of "maleness," his male protagonists vacillate in emotional commitment, as do Romeo and Antony, or lose faith altogether, as does Othello. This disparity between female constancy and male inconstancy within the intimate relationship creates a tension between comic and tragic impulses at the heart of dramas as dissimilar—and similar—as *Romeo and Juliet, Othello,* and *Antony and Cleopatra.*

2

Romeo and Juliet: Female Subjectivity and the Petrarchan Discursive Tradition

> There is no private life which is not determined by a larger public life.
>
> —George Eliot, *Daniel Deronda*

Romeo and Juliet is a play concerned with language, forms, and conventions—a phenomenon not overlooked by critical commentary.[1] Virtuosic poetic passages and set pieces—oxymora, rhymed couplets, sestets, sonnets, an epithalamium, and an *aubade*—stud the play like jewels. While they may obtrude during a private reading upon our absorption with character in action, they enhance our enjoyment of the play in performance. Some commentators dismiss these flourishes as the excesses of a poet as yet undisciplined as a playwright. H. B. Charlton, for example, contends that as a tragedy, *Romeo and Juliet* "is a failure" (1939; 1948, 49–63). Others find significance in the correspondences between the protagonists' passion and the language that conveys it. Nicholas Brooke maintains that the play "is not simply, or so much, an immature play, as a very highly organized play about (among other things) immaturity" (1968, 88). The tragedy is famous for its long arias, as Michael Goldman points out: "the speeches of the lovers are expressions of their isolation and desire; separated from each other, they speak at length" (1972, 40).

Critical approaches to *Romeo and Juliet* which depend upon prescriptive theories of tragedy have largely exhausted themselves; concern with whether the play is a "tragedy of character" or a "tragedy of fate" has ebbed. Those who would point the moral lesson of Friar Lawrence instructing the lovers in moderation sound overly didactic,[2] yet those who would vindicate the protagonists by placing responsibility for the tragic action on an inevitable fate offer an overly deterministic viewpoint.[3] For even in his earliest attempts at tragedy, Shakespeare is capable of managing the delicate balance between choice and chance: Juliet and Romeo are neither condemned by their decisions, as the "tragedy of character" critics would have us believe, nor damned by a mechanical fate, as the "tragedy of fate" critics would have us believe. Incorporating these polarized interpretations allows a consideration of the protagonists' strengths with their weaknesses and a recognition of the feud's power that does not skew it into an inevitable fate. A third major approach, which would have us believe that Shakespeare presents a providential viewpoint,[4] offers the promise of freeing the lovers of both blame and determinism. This view alleges that not Romeo and Juliet but the Montagues and the Capulets are the principals of the tragic action. Its emphasis on divine providence shifts the focus from the death of the lovers to the new harmony between the feuding families. We are asked to believe that the healing of the feud and the restoration of a divine order are of primary concern.

Recent commentators follow Coleridge's view that the lovers are the drama's focus, concentrating not on the play's alleged failures but the aesthetic traits that make it the most frequently performed Shakespearean drama after *Hamlet* (Hibbard 1973, 138). Concerned with the play's structural, thematic, and poetic dualities, Marion Bodwell Smith stresses the play's elemental oppositions; Norman Rabkin examines its manifestation of a Renaissance love-death paradox; Harry Levin emphasizes the play's stylistic symmetries. Whereas Levin distinguishes between the lovers' natural mode of expression and the other characters' formal mode of expression, it is more fruitful to distinguish between Romeo's language and Juliet's. The uniqueness of their poetic styles not only conveys their individual thoughts and emotions but also illuminates the nature of the relationship that defines their lives. Rosalie Colie stands out among those critics who mention in passing either Juliet's directness of expression or her practical nature or her relative maturity: "Juliet, with her language more 'real' than her lover's, is to be taken as the nobler, or more mature, of the two—indeed, in the simplifying of his language, we are to read Romeo's growth through his new love . . . to a mature, even noble, stature, to equal hers" (1974, 166). But no one, I think, fully explores these stylistic and character traits or their implications for the love relationship.

The Chivalric Lover

All three love tragedies open with the culturally familiar derisive views of sex, love, and—whether implicitly as in *Romeo and Juliet* or explicitly as in *Othello* and *Antony and Cleopatra*—the love relationship that will dominate center stage. These opening exchanges

pose a premise that the rest of the play tests: our emotional responses
to the work of art inform our decisions as to which is more valid and
more valuable—the conventional propositions or the extraordinary
relationships that defy them.[5] In the opening scene of *Romeo and
Juliet*, Shakespeare presents in the Capulet servants' ribald exchange
and Romeo's Petrarchan posturing two opposite perspectives on love,
sex, and women. It is no accident that the play in which he first
explores the dynamics of love in a tragic context is one of his most
bawdy plays, for "the bawdy has always a dramatic function," as
Molly Mahood reminds us (1957, 60). The action opens upon Sampson's and Gregory's puns on combat and sex:

> *Sampson.* I will show myself a tyrant: when I have fought with the men, I
>   will be civil with the maids; I will cut off their heads.
> *Gregory.* The heads of the maids?
> *Sampson.* Ay, the heads of the maids, or their maidenheads, take it in what
>   sense thou wilt.
> *Gregory.* They must take it in sense that feel it.
> *Sampson.* Me they shall feel while I am able to stand, and 'tis known I am
>   a pretty piece of flesh.
>
> (1.1.21–29)

The servants present one possible relationship between man and
woman, "a brutal male dominance expressed in sadistic quibbles"
(Mahood 1957, 60). This coarseness of attitude is taken up in the
Nurse's fascination with propagation and Mercutio's antiroman-
ticism, what Maynard Mack calls his "witty resolution of all love into
sex" ([1960] 1970, 327). All three voices provide comic correctives to
the romantic attitudinizing of the early Romeo. Shakespearean tragedy, Mack observes, often employs at least one character, usually
someone in the male protagonist's immediate entourage—servitor,
wife, friend—whose "opposing voice" is juxtaposed to the hyperbole
of the protagonist by its understatement, colloquialism, or deflating
accent ([1960] 1970, 327).

When Romeo appears after the Capulet servants' banter and the
ensuing violence, the chivalric pose replaces the naturalistic tone,
idealizing replaces denigrating, romanticism replaces antiroman-
ticism. He expresses in "the numbers that Petrarch flow'd in"
(2.4.38–39)[6] another possible relationship between man and
woman—the courtly lover's subjection to the tyranny of the cruel fair.
Deliberately set apart from the violence on Verona's streets, as Coleridge notes, he is a young man in love with the idea of being in love:
"Romeo became enamored of the idea he had formed in his own

mind, and then, as it were, christened the first real being of the contrary sex as endowed with the perfections he desired. He appears to be in love with Rosaline, but, in truth, he is in love only with his own idea" ([1960] 1964, 182). His rhetoric and stance are those of the self-absorbed Petrarchan lover who waxes poetic on unrequited love.

If violence provides a natural link between male combat and sex in Sampson's and Gregory's minds, it links the feud with love in Romeo's. Oxymora describing evidence of the street fighting merge seamlessly into oxymora that describe his emotional turmoil:

> Here's much to do with hate, but more with love.
> Why then, O brawling love! O loving hate!
> Of any thing, of nothing first create!
> O heavy lightness, serious vanity,
> Misshapen chaos of well-seeming forms,
> Feather of lead, bright smoke, cold fire, sick health,
> Still-waking sleep, that is not what it is!
> This love feel I, that feel no love in this.
>
> (1.1.175–82)

The feud and love are nearly indistinguishable to him because of their common violence—one disrupts the social equilibrium, the other his own. Significantly, Romeo's oxymoronic catalog is straight out of tradition as the following passage from *Roman de la Rose* makes clear:

> Love is troubled peace, an amorous war—
> A treasonous loyalty, disloyal faith—
> A fear that's full of hope, a desperate trust—
> A madman's logic, reasoned foolishness—
> A pleasant peril in which one may drown—
> A heavy burden that is light to bear—
> Charybdis gracious, threatening overthrow—
> A healthy sickness and most languourous health—
> A famine swallowed up in gluttony—
> A miserly sufficiency of gold—
> A drunken thirst, a thirsty drunkenness—
> A sadness gay, a frolicsomeness sad—
>
> (*Roman de la Rose*, 21.51–62)

Romeo's focus, like that of Elizabethan sonneteers generally, is not on the object of his affections, Rosaline, but on himself: love is a disease; love renders him ill. The poetic attention lavished upon the subject of love barely conceals the more immediate need for self-dramatization:

Love is a smoke made with the fume of sighs,
Being purg'd, a fire sparkling in lovers' eyes,
Being vex'd, a sea nourish'd with loving tears.
What is it else? a madness most discreet,
A choking gall, and a preserving sweet.

(1.1.190–94)

When the unrequited lover shifts the focus from himself to his love object, it is to emphasize her unavailability. Rosaline's vows of chastity make her unavailable; any relationship with her is impossible. Romeo's desire, exacerbated by the impossibility of future conquest, finds expression in the traditional language of love's mythological assault:

> . . . she'll not be hit
With Cupid's arrow, she hath Dian's wit;
And in strong proof of chastity well arm'd,
From Love's weak childish bow she lives uncharm'd.
She will not stay the siege of loving terms,
Nor bide th' encounter of assailing eyes,
Nor ope her lap to saint-seducing gold.

(1.1.208–14)

He combines slave-like devotion to Rosaline with an attack on her chastity. "Love is a man of war," Mahood notes, "in such phrases as 'th' encounter of assailing eyes,'" adding to Sampson's and Gregory's aggressive wordplay (1957, 60). Underlying Petrarchan discourse lies a concern with sexual conquest and possession not unlike that made explicit by Ovidian discourse. Lovemaking in both lyric and narrative courtly literature is consistently represented, as Joseph Boone maintains, as a siege or battle (1987, 41). The whole allegorical premise of *Roman de la Rose,* in fact, concluding in the lover's climactic assault on the "castle" of Belacueil's chastity, simultaneously describes the sexual act in the language of religion and equates it with the violence of war:

A little then I pushed aside the shroud
That curtained the fair relics, and approached
The image that I knew was close within.
Devotedly I kissed the sacred place.
Safely to sheathe my staff within the shrine,
I thrust it through the loophole, while the scrip
Dangled behind it. Carefully I tried
To thrust it in; it bounded back again.
Once again I thrust it in without avail;

Always it back recoiled. Try as I might,
Nothing could force the staff to enter there.
Then I perceived a little barricade,
Which though I well could feel I could not see,
Quite near the border of the opening,
Which from the inside fortified the shrine,
Having been placed there when it first was made,
And still remained fast and quite secure.
More vigorously then I made assault;
But often as I thrust, so oft I failed.

(Roman de la Rose, 99.203–21)

The procreation argument is a familiar one from the most conventional of Shakespeare's sonnets where the beloved is male, as Joseph Pequigney maintains (1985, passim). Here, though, it is but a guise for the attempt to gain sexual satisfaction. The fact of human mortality condemns Rosaline's beauty to transience: "O, she is rich in beauty, only poor / That, when she dies, with beauty dies her store" (1.1.215–16). In denying her sexuality she denies perpetuation of her beauty: "For beauty starv'd with her severity / Cuts beauty off from all posterity" (1.1.219–20). Romeo's rhetoric here, as earlier however, pales in comparison to the conquest of maidenhead so graphically described in *Roman de la Rose*.

Benvolio's realistic suggestion of the greater possibility for mutuality presented by other women prompts Romeo to a hyperbolic vow of loyalty to Rosaline. His one-sided worship, employing standard religious imagery and taking the shape of the traditional sestet, is precisely commensurate with her beauty:

When the devout religion of mine eye
Maintains such falsehood, then turn tears to fires;
And these, who, often drown'd, could never die,
Transparent heretics, be burnt for liars!
One fairer than my love! The all-seeing sun
Ne'er saw her match since first the world begun.

(1.2.88–93)

So committed is he to physical beauty that he is a "devout" follower of the "religion of [his] eye." His emphasis on "eye" as a detector of beauty rather than as a window into the soul of the beloved reveals his concern with the outer, not the inner. It is significant that we see Rosaline exclusively through Romeo's eyes and that she has no independent existence in the world of the play. Her absence accentuates his placement of affection on the unavailable and the impossible. As long as Romeo depends upon Petrarchan conventions, both he and his silent, passive beloved are locked in a stance that allows only unilateral expression and prevents not only mutual devotion, but any interaction at all between man and woman.[7]

His verbal extravagance is sometimes omitted in performance, by Franco Zeffirelli, for example. But it is significant because—like the "taffeta phrases" that Berowne and Navarre speak in their movement from vows of celibacy to vows of marriage—it emphasizes the departure point from which he matures. His utter conventionality in love places him firmly within the chivalric tradition. Lewis, in his discussion of the lover in *Roman de la Rose*, describes the familiar situation awaiting the courtly lover: "when a young man recognizes that he is 'in love,' he may well feel that he has come to a place where others have come before him, a place with laws of its own that existed before he met them, in which certain things, not unknown from literature and tradition, are now to be done and suffered" ([1936] 1958, 130). Elizabethans, of course, were well aware of this tradition, and as Lisle John points out, "took for granted a definite code of action as a manifestation of the symptoms and effects of love" (quoted in Levenson 1982, 24). As Jill Levenson puts it, "Romeo embodies that code" (1982, 24). *Romeo and Juliet* dramatizes the male protagonist's movement beyond the confines of tradition and his quest into unknown psychological terrain, freed of conventions:

> He that hath the steerage of my course
> Direct my sail!
>
> (1.4.112–13)

>   I am no pilot, yet, wert thou as far
> As that vast shore wash'd with the farthest sea,
> I should adventure for such merchandise.
>
> (2.2.82–84)

>   Thou desperate pilot, now at once run on
> The dashing rocks thy sea-sick weary bark!
>
> (5.3.117–18)

His several metaphorical references to sea voyages, though drawn from the Petrarchan arsenal, emphasize this inner journey.

Juliet as Comic Protagonist

We are introduced to Juliet in a very few lines. Yet in the brief exchange with the Nurse and her mother, Juliet exhibits, as Nicholas

Brooke notes, "a fuller humanity than Romeo has yet displayed"
(1968, 93). Incapable of acting out the stereotypical role of the adoles-
cent female languishing for a lover, she is instead a marriageable
daughter whose parents are choosing a husband. Her first words
convey indifference to the idea of "honorable" arranged marriage: "It
is an honor that I dream not of" (1.3.66). The artificiality of her
mother's set piece on Paris lies not only in its extended metaphor of
Paris as a book but in its conventional valuation of physical beauty
and material wealth:

> Read o'er the volume of young Paris' face
> And find delight writ there with beauty's pen. . . .
> So shall you share all that he doth possess,
> By having him, making yourself no less.
>
> (1.3.81–94)

Juliet's concise answer, "I'll look to like," would exemplify obedience
were it not for the conditional clause, "if looking liking move"
(1.3.97) that calls into question any automatic cause-and-effect relationship between the beauty and wealth of Paris and emotional commitment on her part.

We know Romeo and Juliet are suited to one another because
Shakespeare establishes their immediate rapport in the repartée of
their sonnet exchange. They are of like mind. "Romeo has met his
match," as Brooke puts it (1968, 96). At his first sight of her he echoes
the stance of one-sided worship of Rosaline in even more richly
conceited language:

> O, she doth teach the torches to burn bright!
> It seems she hangs upon the cheek of night
> As a rich jewel in an Ethiop's ear—
> Beauty too rich for use, for earth too dear!
>
> (1.5.44–47)

Juliet demands of him, however, active engagement. She turns his
poetic overture into the second quatrain of a sonnet, making a joke of
his conventional religion of love. She expands on his imagery—his
lips as pilgrims worshipping at the shrine of her hand—but gently
puts him in his place, granting him permission to touch her hand "in
prayer," but not to kiss it:

> *Romeo.* If I profane with my unworthiest hand
>   This holy shrine, the gentle sin is this,
>   My lips, two blushing pilgrims, ready stand

To smooth that rough touch with a tender kiss.
Juliet. Good pilgrim, you do wrong your hand too much,
   Which mannerly devotion shows in this:
   For saints have hands that pilgrims' hands do touch,
   And palm to palm is holy palmers' kiss.

                                                                 (1.5.93–100)

In psychological terms, as Brooke notes, their sonnet exchange represents "the spell of mutual recognition" (1968, 95). The formal symmetry of their exchange, one quatrain spoken by Romeo, the next by Juliet, gives way in the third quatrain to a faster-paced, quick-witted interaction of simultaneous attack and counterattack, attraction and counterattraction:

Romeo. Have not saints lips, and holy palmers too?
Juliet. Ay, pilgrim, lips that they must use in pray'r.
Romeo. O then, dear saint, let lips do what hands do,
   They pray—grant thou, lest faith turn to despair.
Juliet. Saints do not move, though grant for prayers' sake.
Romeo. Then move not while my prayer's effect I take.
   Thus from my lips, by thine, my sin is purg'd.
Juliet. Then have my lips the sin that they have took.
Romeo. Sin from my lips? O trespass sweetly urg'd!
   Give me my sin again.
Juliet.   You kiss by th' book.

                                                                 (1.5.101–10)

They punctuate the couplet and the extra quatrain with a kiss. Her mocking commentary, "You kiss by th' book," one of several references to doing things by the book in this formal society,[8] gently brings him down to earth. In Shakespeare's comedies, Marianne Novy observes, witty repartée between lovers often suggests the potential for a deeper compatibility: "much of each play develops the characters' relationships before they directly offer and ask love; instead, they ask and yield response to wit and verbal style. The linguistic mutuality . . . differs from emotional mutuality but hints at this possibility" (1984, 23–24). Beatrice and Benedick, of course, immediately come to mind. In *Romeo and Juliet*, however, the lovers' witty exchange expresses rather than merely suggests their mutual devotion at the very moment they meet. Their reciprocal exchange caps the movement of act 1 from "sonneteering as mere attitudinizing," as Brooke puts it, to the "sonnet as formal embodiment of valid feeling" (1968, 96).
   It is remarkable that in the most celebrated love scene in western

literature, the lovemaking is at a physical remove, its powerful effect achieved through the magic of language. Less remarked upon is the fact that the orchard scene is one of the most humorous in Shakespeare, the humor being created by the disparity in the concerns and language of the lovers: Romeo is romantic, incapable of practicality; Juliet, practical, incapable of romantic rhetoric. Of the drama's twenty-four scenes, Shakespeare gives them parts of four together: they exchange a mere eighteen lines at the Capulet feast; eleven lines at Friar Lawrence's cell; fifty-five lines at their departure. The orchard scene, the lengthiest of their exchanges, offers the most ample opportunity for the audience to witness their interaction with one another and Juliet tutoring Romeo in love. Romeo's "lessoning in the school of love is superbly done," Karl Thompson notes; "as a demonstration of the art of wooing there can be none better" (1971, 74). One reason the scene is so very pleasurable and memorable is that the lovers are as suffused in Juliet's good-natured generosity as the tangible moonlight.

When Romeo sees Juliet at her window his Marlovian hyperbole describes her beauty in an extended invidious, metaphorical comparison:

> But soft! what light through yonder window breaks?
> It is the east, and Juliet is the sun.
> Arise, fair sun, and kill the envious moon,
> Who is already sick and pale with grief
> That thou, her maid, art far more fair than she.
> Be not her maid, since she is envious;
> Her vestal livery is but sick and green,
> And none but fools do wear it; cast it off.
>
> (2.2.2–9)

The ethereal talk of "sun," "moon," "stars," and "angels" beginning with this passage reveals more about his ecstatic state of mind than anything about Juliet. In his continued dependence on sonnet conventions, in his wish, "O that I were a glove upon that hand, / That I might touch that cheek!" (2.2.24–25), he is not unlike the Romeo of the opening scene.

Juliet, however, is of a different mind. As though having no thought since their meeting but the obstacle between them—"My only love sprung from my only hate! / Too early seen unknown, and known too late"(1.5.138–39)—she takes up where she left off upon learning Romeo's identity as a Montague. Entirely unconcerned with what absorbs Romeo's attention—the idealization of the physical—

her concern is the practical one of their dilemma: "wherefore art thou
Romeo? / Deny thy father and refuse thy name" (2.2.33–34). As
Michael Goldman notes, "Romeo's name presents a problem to
others besides Juliet but she characteristically sees more deeply into
the difficulty" (1972, 35). Her attempt at a solution is a mutual one
that demands no more of Romeo than of herself: "Or, if thou wilt
not, be but sworn my love, / And I'll no longer be a Capulet"
(2.2.35–36). We have no sense that she indulges in excess: her directness of statement and intimacy of tone convince us of her sincerity
of feeling, that indeed she would forsake her name and her family for
him. Grappling with the emotional conflict between family loyalty
and love, she distinguishes his nonessential "name" from his essential
"self":[9]

> 'Tis but thy name that is my enemy;
> Thou art thyself, though not a Montague.
> What's Montague? It is nor hand nor foot,
> Nor arm nor face, nor any other part
> Belonging to a man. O, be some other name!
> What's in a name? That which we call a rose
> By any other word would smell as sweet;
> So Romeo would, were he not Romeo call'd,
> Retain that dear perfection which he owes
> Without that title.
>
> (2.2.38–47)

In so doing, as Harry Levin points out, she calls into question "not
merely Romeo's name but—by implication—all names, forms, conventions, sophistications, and arbitrary dictates of society" ([1960]
1970, 280). Her insistence on the supremacy of his "dear perfection"
to his "title" inverts the sonnet convention of anatomizing the lover:
the name Montague "is nor hand nor foot, / Nor arm nor face, nor
any other part."

Juliet's awareness of her emotional state is matched by her
awareness of the danger posed by the feud. Once Romeo emerges
from the shadows, her direct practical questions consistently puncture his effusive romantic declarations. The two lovers speak two
different languages:

> *Juliet.* How camest thou hither, tell me, and wherefore?
>   The orchard walls are high and hard to climb,
>   And the place death, considering who thou art,
>   If any of my kinsmen find thee here.
> *Romeo.* With love's light wings did I o'erperch these walls,

For stony limits cannot hold love out. . . .
Juliet. If they do see the, they will murther thee.
Romeo. Alack, there lies more peril in thine eye
    Than twenty thousand of their swords! . . .
Juliet. I would not for the world they saw thee here.
Romeo. I have night's cloak to hide me from their eyes. . . .
Juliet. By whose direction foundst thou out this place?
Romeo. By Love, that first did prompt me to inquire;
    He lent me counsel, and I lent him eyes.

(2.2.62–81)

Mistrusting his responses, indeed seeming to put no stock in them at all, she asks him, rather pointedly, "Dost thou love me?" (2.2.90). Her emphasis on faith, "If thou dost love, pronounce it faithfully" (2.2.94), reveals her suspicion that his declarations lack substance and her desire that he find the truth within himself and speak not in clichés, but simply, from the heart.[10] Indeed, in lieu of poetic extravagance, one heartfelt monosyllable, "Ay," would suffice: "I know thou wilt say, 'Ay,' / And I will take thy word" (2.2.90–91). She looks for evidence that Romeo's words are true, or "relevant," and that he actually experiences what he says.[11] Her interruption of his vow of love "by yonder blessed moon" emphasizes the point:

O, swear not by the moon, th' inconstant moon,
That monthly changes in her circled orb,
Lest that thy love prove likewise variable. . . .
                Do not swear at all;
Or if thou wilt, swear by thy gracious self.

(2.2.109–13)

Her confidence in the integrity of his "gracious self" matches her confidence in herself. Understanding her own emotions and intuiting the same in him, Juliet proposes to Romeo: "If that thy bent of love be honorable, / Thy purpose marriage, send me word to-morrow" (2.2.143–44). In so doing, she anticipates Desdemona's similar violation of social convention in initiating courtship with Othello. And because Juliet has just told Romeo, "Fain would I dwell on form. . . . / I'll prove more true / Than those that have more coying to be strange" (2.2.88–101), we are not surprised.

Spontaneity and simplicity characterize her expression of emotions of "boundless" breath and depth. Language falls short of the task for Cordelia: "my love's / More ponderous than my tongue. . . . I cannot heave / My heart into my mouth" (*King Lear*, 1.1.77–92). Language expands, however, to fit the power of Juliet's feelings. The infinitude of her love, rather than finding language inadequate, finds eloquent expression. Her quintessential expression of her love is as remarkable for its emphasis on giving as its intensity of feeling:

> My bounty is as boundless as the sea,
> My love as deep; the more I give to thee,
> The more I have, for both are infinite.

(2.2.133–35)

The image, although erotic, is the emotional climax of the scene because of its emphasis on active generosity—love is an infinitely renewing force that paradoxically defies logical expectations of something being decreased by being given away. Juliet thus anticipates Desdemona's similar understanding of love as a dynamic creative force that she reveals when she insists on its capacity for growth: "The heavens forbid / But that our loves and comfort should increase / Even as our days do grow!" (Othello, 2.1.193–95). All that follows in this scene, including the arrangements for marriage, which are mentioned almost as an afterthought, is denouement to Juliet's deeply felt and beautifully expressed emotion. Her capacity for naturalness and ease of expression, moreover, make her critical of studied, carefully crafted phrases of love. When Romeo asks that she proclaim her joy at their wedding, she echoes Rosaline and the Princess tutoring Berowne and Navarre in the relationship between love and language: "Conceit, more rich in matter than in words, / Brags of his substance, not of ornament" (2.6.30–31). When she continues, "They are but beggars that can count their worth," she suggests, like Antony, "There's beggary in the love that can be reckon'd" (Antony and Cleopatra, 1.1.15), refusal rather than inability to quantify love in language.

In Othello and Antony and Cleopatra there is nothing like the orchard scene where the female protagonist tutors the male protagonist in love. Whereas Desdemona's initiation of courtship and Cleopatra's reciprocation of Antony's dinner invitation are recent or distant actions recollected, Juliet's refusal to play the role of Romeo's Petrarchan love object and her proposal of marriage dominate center stage.[12] It is Juliet's good-natured generosity that differentiates the scene from the brittleness of Love's Labor's tutorial sessions. The humor of the scene derives largely, as we have seen, from her practice of deflating Romeo's romantic hyperboles, yet it culminates in a misunderstanding on her part. She responds to what she thinks is an assault by Romeo on her chastity: "wilt thou leave me so unsatisfied?" (2.2.125). In doing so, she reveals her awareness of the concern with sexual possession that underlies the Petrarchan stance: "What satisfaction canst thou have to-night?" (2.2.126). But as Romeo soon makes clear, the only satisfaction he is seeking is vows, while her response reveals (although inadvertently) that she is thinking of sexual satisfaction. Juliet's awareness of sexuality, which is given full expression in her epithalamium, is introduced in this innocent, humorous context. This expression of sexual candor both reiterates that of the female protagonists of Shakespeare's comedies and anticipates that of Desdemona before the Venetian Senate: "if I be left behind, / A moth of peace, and he go to the war, / The rites for why I love him are bereft me" (*Othello*, 1.3.255–57).

Because the marriage is secret, it does not strike us that Shakespeare alters literary tradition when Juliet, not the wedding guests of convention, speaks the epithalamium.[13] She "unknowingly inverts tradition," as Jill Levenson puts it (1982, 30); she is not fearful of the wedding night. Indeed, where the groom usually voices desire, she joyously proclaims hers: "I have bought the mansion of a love, / But not possess'd it, and though I am sold, / Not yet enjoy'd" (3.2.26–28). This candid reiteration of her love's bounty emphasizes its reciprocal nature as well: both lovers partake of "buying" and "selling" as well as "possessing" and "enjoying" love's passion. Love and passion are one; "this *is* desire," Brooke insists, "recognized and focused as it must be at that point where love and lust are identical" (1968, 101). Yet this attitude and expression are quite removed from the conventional reduction of love to lust that is voiced by the antiromantic stance—lightheartedly, in the comic tradition, by Mercutio, and later, with tragic consequences, by Iago. Not Romeo but Juliet performs the rite of banishing daylight and welcoming darkness:

> Come, civil night,
> Thou sober-suited matron all in black,
> And learn me how to lose a winning match,
> Play'd for a pair of stainless maidenhoods.
>
> (3.2.10–13)

Consummation is, therefore, imagined not in the customary masculine language of conquest but as a *reciprocal* game of risk, venturing, or quest. Both lovers, "a pair of maidenhoods," "lose" their innocence as they "win" their pleasure. Despite the metaphor, it is clear that this is no game for Juliet. She speaks here, as always, from her heart. If sexual desire as expressed by Juliet in act 3 were omitted but sexual desire as expressed by Romeo in act 1 were included, our response to its expression in the play would be less sympathetic than it is. Not only does she voice desire "with a new intensity quite removed from the innocent romantic stuff we have had earlier," as Brooke points out (1968, 83), but her confidence in the integrity of their "gracious selves" and her insistence on mutual interaction—despite her awareness of the emotional vulnerability involved—make possible a love that surpasses narcissistic desire and its failure to connect with the reality of the other.

The Chivalric Avenger

Tybalt's, Mercutio's, and finally Romeo's adherence to the code of revenge obviously acts at cross-purposes to the connection the two protagonists make with one another and reaffirm despite their knowledge of familial enmity. At the very moment Romeo and Juliet meet one another at the Capulet feast, Tybalt takes offense at Romeo's presence. The feast thus serves as the origin of the revenge plot that intensifies in the second street fighting scene (3.1) and concludes in the final duel (5.3), and the love story that intensifies in the orchard scene (2.2) and concludes in the Capulet vault (5.3). These key scenes reveal the change in Romeo. In the street fighting scene he plays the role of chivalric avenger; in the orchard scene he plays the role of chivalric lover.[14] In the final duel with Paris and in the Capulet vault with Juliet, he plays neither role.

Romeo's relationship to Tybalt is somewhat similar to Hamlet's relationship to Laertes: both male protagonists are reluctant avengers who must confront more eager avengers as enemy. The tragedy of *Hamlet* is that the male protagonist dies at the moment he is fit to be king. Despite his transcendence of the revenge code, his world is governed by it. Like Hamlet at his duel with Laertes, Romeo at his duel with Paris has surpassed the code of revenge. *Romeo and Juliet* would be a comedy if Romeo were challenged merely to break through the boundaries of his role as chivalric lover because Juliet successfully tutors him in the realm of intimate relations. But the play is a tragedy because he is challenged to break out of his role as chivalric avenger as well, and Juliet's effect upon him is insufficient in this sphere. *Romeo and Juliet* is a tragedy instead of a comedy because Romeo kills Tybalt before he breaks out of the role of avenger.

After their initial appearances, neither Montague nor Capulet seems committed to perpetuating the feud between the two households. Montague sounds regretful: "Who set this ancient quarrel new abroach?" (1.1.104); Capulet sounds hopeful: " 'tis not hard, I think,

/ For men so old as we to keep the peace" (1.2.1–3). Hospitality, not enmity, is Capulet's overriding concern when he learns of Romeo's presence at the Capulet feast. The virulence of the feud, far from being kindled by the two patriarchs is, as James Calderwood puts it, mitigated by two "spindle-shanked and slippered old men who allow the feud to continue less from rancor than from apathy" ([1971] 1984, 46). The perpetuation of the feud does not depend upon the inclinations of the two patriarchs, then. Having attained the desired status and prestige conferred by marriage, children, wealth, social position, and age, they are reluctant to continue it. The extent to which they are responsible lies in their curious blend of indulgence and negligence—authoritarian behavior within the home (at least in the case of Capulet) and abrogation of responsibility outside it.

The perpetuation of the feud depends upon the inclinations of the young, for it is a rite of passage in Verona.[15] Sampson, Gregory, Abraham, Balthasar, Tybalt, and Mercutio believe in it and perpetuate it because they are immature and therefore have a stake in proving themselves to be men, as the opening scenes of act 1 and act 3 make clear. Such participation guarantees the feud's cyclic continuation from one generation to the next: when one generation matures beyond its dictates, the next takes its place. Capulet's and Tybalt's quarrel at the feast underscores this generational disparity in attitudes toward enforcing the feud. Although verbal bantering escalates to physical violence at the play's outset, the predominant comic atmosphere of the first two acts prevents further escalation to the point of death. The danger of testing limits of tolerance with insults and playing at the razor's edge between life and death is quite enough risk taking to confer status on the youths in each other's eyes.[16] The problem arises when the violence veers out of control.

The injunction of the comedies, that one "must give and hazard all he hath" (*The Merchant of Venice*, 2.7.9), is thus perverted in this comedy turned tragedy. Romeo tries to "hazard all" in love, but he is surrounded by young males who prefer to "hazard all" in antagonism toward one another rather than in affection for a member of the opposite sex—in the violence they take as evidence of their masculinity rather than behavior that subordinates the stereotypically masculine to a broader, deeper, fuller humanity. Romeo's participation in risk taking is different in kind from the violence of the feud: he violates social taboo in joining his peers at the Capulet feast in act 1 and in "o'erperching" the walls of the Capulet orchard in act 2.

Even as Romeo's infatuation with Rosaline sets him apart from the street fighting at the outset of the play, his love for Juliet sets him apart from it at the outset of act 3. When he enters fresh from his marriage vows to Juliet, he does indeed seem "new baptiz'd" (2.2.50). His tone is matter-of-fact, much as it was that morning when his altered demeanor elicited Mercutio's unwittingly accurate response, "now art thou Romeo, now art thou what thou art" (2.6.89–90), although the cause for the transformation remains a mystery to the high-spirited antiromantic. In contrast to his peers' indulgence in emotional excess, Romeo's composure is all the more apparent, as D. A. Traversi notes: "in the midst of so much unreason, it is only Romeo, in his new situation, who expresses himself with realism to the man who insists in regarding himself as his mortal enemy" ([1956] 1969, 124). In denying Tybalt's charge, Romeo, although he conceals his marriage, twice insists on subordinating the dictates of the feud to the new connection between them:

> Tybalt, the reason that I have to love thee
> Doth much excuse the appertaining rage
> To such a greeting. Villain am I none;
> Therefore farewell, I see thou knowest me not. . . .
> I do protest I never injuried thee,
> But love thee better than thou canst devise,
> Till thou shalt know the reason of my love,
> And so, good Capulet—which name I tender
> As dearly as my own—be satisfied.
>
> (3.1.62–72)

Romeo's assertion, "thou knowest me not," reiterates Juliet's earlier insistence on the supremacy of personal integrity to familial enmity. Because Mercutio shares with Tybalt an incomprehension of Romeo's sentiments and a sensitivity to the dishonor of "reputation stain'd," it is not surprising that not Romeo but he should respond to Tybalt. Comic tilts to tragic on the fulcrum of Mercutio's and Tybalt's only confrontation; their common concern with honor and the code of revenge allows their clashing egos to force the violence of the feud to obtrude upon the love story.

While Romeo is preoccupied with his relationship to Tybalt through his marriage to Juliet rather than any distinction from him, he has no care of any stain upon his reputation from "Tybalt's slander." There are echoes of the courtly tradition in Romeo's be-havior, as Thompson reminds us: "Romeo, behaving correctly while he endures the taunts of the jeering Tybalt, is undergoing the trial, like Chrétien's knights, of bearing ignominy and loss of honor for the sake of the lady" (1971, 75). But so great is Romeo's shock, even guilt, at Mercutio's death "on [his] behalf" that he eschews the influence of marriage and love: "O sweet Juliet, / Thy beauty hath made me effeminate / And in my temper soft'ned valor's steel!" (3.1.113–15). He adopts Mercutio's and Tybalt's rhetoric of honor as he assumes the quid pro quo burden of the code of revenge:

> He gone in triumph, and Mercutio slain!
> Away to heaven, respective lenity,
> And fire-ey'd fury be my conduct now!
> Now, Tybalt, take the villain back again
> That late thou gavest me; for Mercutio's soul
> Is but a little way above our heads,
> Staying for thine to keep him company.
> Either thou or I, or both, must go with him.
>
> (3.1.122–29)

Had he greater capacity for deliberation, perhaps, Romeo might allow Escalus to mete out the punishment Tybalt deserves, but instead the proclamation of banishment that should fall on Tybalt falls on him. To put revenge and honor above love is to betray the code of love, Thompson notes, and thus causes the ensuing disaster (1971, 75).

Just as Juliet's love initiates Romeo into the private realm of authentic emotional commitment, Mercutio's death initiates him into the public world of the feud. As though rehearsing for love, Romeo as idolator of Rosaline creates a world of "artificial night." But he has no like preparation for Mercutio's death because he never participates, as do his peers, in the rehearsal for death that is street fighting. Under the influence of Juliet's love he begins to shed role playing as he begins to act from his innermost self. The irony of his being drawn into the feud by acting from his heart does not escape us. Romeo would be true to the courtly code if he endured even the death of his friend for his lady's sake. It is not at the Capulet's feast, or beneath Juliet's balcony, that he breaks with the courtly code, but when he sets off in pursuit of Tybalt (Thompson 1971, 75). We might be tempted to view Romeo as abandoning one chivalric role, that of self-dramatizing lover, only to adopt another, that of self-righteous avenger, were it not for his capacity for feeling shown both in his connection with Juliet and in his contrast to his peers. He does not merely act out the dictates of a code as do both Mercutio and Tybalt. Rather, he does give in to cultural pressures that he fight, but because personal relationships are of as supreme importance to him as they are to Juliet, he does so only after an extreme impetus—the death of his best friend. Mercutio and Tybalt die learning neither the unworthiness of the code that circumscribes their existence nor the value of love. The emphasis on their rash behavior and shallow natures, in their primary function as foils to Romeo, mitigates the effect of his killing Tybalt and heightens our sense of Romeo's capacity for feeling. Shakespeare shifts the focus from the male code of vengeance to the more universal experience of the unbearable pain of loss when he represents as Romeo's motive not wounded honor, but grief.

Juliet as Tragic Protagonist

It is quite natural that Juliet should dominate the tragedy throughout acts 3 and 4. She undergoes one crisis after another from the very moment Romeo departs. One abandonment after another— by her father, her mother, the Nurse, and finally, Friar Lawrence— exacerbates the effect of her separation from him. Reaching out for help and finding none, she is forced back upon her self into a stance of self-reliance by her increasing isolation and the quick succession of events: Tybalt's death; Romeo's banishment; an arranged marriage become an enforced marriage; a sleeping potion she fears is a death potion; and Romeo's death.

While we may be tempted to view Shakespeare's representation of youthful heterosexual relations as so idealistic as to preclude any alienation of the lovers from one another, this is not what he represents in *Romeo and Juliet*. Each protagonist experiences estrangement, albeit momentary, from the other. Romeo's "Juliet, / Thy beauty hath made me effeminate" constitutes the turning point of the dramatic action from comic to tragic, as we have seen. Juliet's discovery of her cousin's death by her husband's hand marks her reaction to this pivotal action of his:

> O serpent heart, hid with a flow'ring face!
> Did ever dragon keep so fair a cave?
> Beautiful tyrant! fiend angelical!
> Dove-feather'd raven! wolvish ravening lamb!
> Despised substance of divinest show!
> Just opposite to what thou justly seem'st,
> A damned saint, an honorable villain!

> (3.2.73–79)

If plain language earlier conveys her certainty in establishing the supremacy of Romeo's "self" to his "name," then artifice conveys her only moment of doubt and her inability to distinguish between his "despised substance" and his "divinest show." Her mind, under pressure, springs loose the oxymoron from its decorative function; her last epithet of the series articulates the dramatic paradox of the play's peripeteia—Romeo's surrender to the dictates of the feud does make him "an honorable villain" indeed.

Juliet's characteristic monosyllabic utterance cuts to the quick of experience, consistently piercing false speech, false perception, and false emotion. The oxymoronic epithets that convey her estrangement from Romeo give way seconds later to simpler expression that conveys solidarity with him: "Blister'd be thy tongue / For such a wish! he was not born to shame" (3.2.90–91). The illusion of the nightingale, sustained throughout the duet of the lovers' *aubade* that complements the aria of her epithalamium, is broken by her return to reality: "It is the lark that sings so out of tune" (3.5.27). Her minimal expression of cold anger, "Speak'st thou from thy heart? . . . / Thou and my bosom henceforth shall be twain" (3.5.226–40), accentuates her maturation to the point she can act alone when betrayed by the Nurse. The artifice of stichomythy that conveys her dissembling stance with Paris gives way to plain monosyllables that reveal her desperation to Friar Lawrence: "O, shut the door, and when thou hast done so, / Come weep with me, past hope, past cure, past help!" (4.1.44–45).

The protagonists' separate crises in act 3 follow naturally from their initial indifference toward "honorable" fighting and "honorable" marriage in act 1. Romeo's reluctance to fight only draws him into the feud: his attempt to stop the street fighting instead involves him in it. Juliet's reluctance to marry only propels her into an arranged marriage: her refusal to obey Capulet instead strengthens his resolve. Both lovers react as best they can in the face of overwhelming forces. Romeo cannot possibly foresee that staying Mercutio's hand will cause his death. Juliet cannot possibly foresee that refusing to comply with Capulet's well-intended plan will cause its calcification into authoritarian determination, transforming the social convention of arranged marriage into an inescapable prison of enforced marriage. Both protagonists finally do act in compliance with Verona's expectations of its young men and women, but only under the extreme duress of Mercutio's death and the threat of banishment from Capulet's house. Yet Romeo's singular public crisis creates an impression of his loss of resolve, of his being overpowered by a social situation he cannot control, while Juliet's several private crises create an impression of her increasing strength in isolation despite similar cultural forces acting upon her. It would be overstating the case to suggest that he acts irrationally while she acts rationally to find a way out of an impossible situation. Romeo's surrender to cultural dictates that he fight does occur somewhat readily, however, in contrast to Juliet's complicated efforts to disentangle herself from cultural dictates that she marry a man not of her choosing, and commit bigamy in doing so.

Shakespeare dramatizes Juliet's isolation in both of her death scenes. Her fear that Friar Lawrence's sleeping potion is a death potion and her graphic imaginings on the green corpses within the Capulet tomb underscore the courage of her actions by emphasizing the obstacles she must overcome to cooperate in his scheme: "Romeo! Here's drink—I drink to thee" (4.3.58). Her last turn to her elders for comfort—"I'll call them back again to comfort me. / Nurse!" (4.3.17–18)—immediately gives way to self-reliance: "—What should she do here? / My dismal scene I needs must act alone" (4.3.18–19). It comes as no shock, therefore, that she responds with complete calm to Friar Lawrence's abandonment of her in the Capulet tomb. Romeo dies alone moments before Friar Lawrence's entrance and Juliet dies alone moments after his exit—two instances of dramaturgical timing that further emphasize the isolation of the protagonists. The coward-ice of Friar Lawrence's departure, "I dare no longer stay" (5.3.159), could not accentuate Juliet's courage more. Her discovery of Romeo's corpse is remarkable for the complete humanity conveyed in her lack of overt anguish. The comic strains running through the tragedy culminate in an uncommon humor that discloses the intimacy be-tween them: "O churl, drunk all, and left no friendly drop / To help me after?" (5.3.163–64). To observe that there is absolutely no quality of self-dramatization or self-pity at the moment of her death is to belabor the obvious. The emotional density of minimal utterance heightens the effect of her death. Her last words are richly meta-phoric, but brief: "O happy dagger, / This is thy sheath; there rust, and let me die" (5.3.169–70).

Breaking Boundaries

Shakespearean journeys, Mack observes, serve either as an outward manifestation of inward change or as a shorthand indication that such change is about to begin or end. They can enhance our impression that "psychological changes are taking place, either by emphasizing a lapse of time, or by taking us to new settings, or by both" ([1960] 1970, 344). Although Shakespeare does not step-by-step trace the psychological development of Hamlet, for example, the man who returns from England is different from the youth who departed. We see something of the same thing, I think, when we see Romeo in Mantua for the first time since his departure from Verona. We do not know whether or how he may have changed until we hear a meditative man, not a whining youth, contemplating his fate. The new tone is completely lacking in self-dramatization and self-pity:

If I may trust the flattering truth of sleep,
My dreams presage some joyful news at hand.
My bosom's lord sits lightly in his throne,
And all this day an unaccustom'd spirit
Lifts me above the ground with cheerful thoughts.
I dreamt my lady came and found me dead—
Strange dream, that gives a dead man leave to think!—
And breath'd such life with kisses in my lips
That I reviv'd and was an emperor.
Ah me, how sweet is love itself possess'd,
When but love's shadows are so rich in joy!

(5.1.1–11)

The dream itself is the stuff of Petrarchan convention, as Levenson notes (1982, 32), but Romeo is untormented by it. Detached enough to smile at himself, commenting whimsically on the dream's "strange" paradox—it allows the capacity for thought to a dead man—he anticipates in his reflectiveness Antony's reverie on "a cloud that's dragonish" (*Antony and Cleopatra*, 4.14.2). The poignancy of the change in Romeo is that in his new maturity is also the suggestion of readiness for death.

Prepared for in only eleven lines, Romeo's response to the news of Juliet's death is his great moment. Because he has been thinking that he will not see her again, he is, remarkably, not shocked: "Is it e'en so?" (5.1.24). In few words he conveys at once macabre humor and quiet gravity: "Well, Juliet, I will lie with thee to-night" (5.1.34). No longer indecisive, he acts. Calm detachment allows his recollection of the incredible detail of the apothecary's shop; his newfound confidence manifests itself as determination to die next to Juliet. If the beginning of act 5 is omitted as is sometimes done (by Zeffirelli, for example), Juliet strikes us as a tragic protagonist, but Romeo does not.

Romeo's intimacy of tone and maturity is accentuated by contrast with the vague, undirected "proliferation of accusations" and self-pity that mark Paris's response:[17]

Beguil'd, divorced, wronged, spited, slain!
Most detestable Death, by thee beguil'd,
By cruel cruel thee quite overthrown!
O love, O life! not life, but love in death!

(4.5.55–58)

Our impression of Romeo's grim determination, together with the
momentum of act 5, prevents us from viewing him as a murderer
when he kills Paris. His confrontation with Paris pits a self-pro-
claimed "madman" whose single aim is to die next to Juliet—"Good
gentle youth, tempt not a desp'rate man" (5.3.59)—against a romantic whose utterly conventional sestet anticipates Claudio at Hero's
tomb in *Much Ado* even more so than it echoes the early Romeo:

> Sweet flower, with flowers thy bridal bed I strew,
> O woe, thy canopy is dust and stones!—
> Which with sweet water nightly I will dew,
> Or wanting that, with tears distill'd by moans.
> The obsequies that I for thee will keep
> Nightly shall be to strew thy grave and weep.
>
> (5.3.12–17)

Shakespeare often represents on stage, toward the close of a tragedy,
what Mack calls "the central dialogue of tragic experience." This key
exchange can be traced from the Greek dialogue of protagonist with
chorus to the seventeenth-century dialogue of soul with body to the
twentieth-century dialogue of self with soul. It is a dialogue in which
"each party makes its case in its own tongue, incapable of wholly
comprehending what the other means," an encounter of "those by
whom, 'changed, changed utterly,' a terrible beauty has been born,"
with "those who are still players in life's casual comedy" ([1960] 1970,
332). Tybalt's earlier confrontation with Romeo imposes tragic ideals
of male honor and revenge upon an essentially comic love plot. Paris's
confrontation with Romeo emphasizes his own confinement within
the comic conventionality of the chivalric lover and Romeo's breaking
through the boundaries of that role. We might feel more moved by
Paris's death than we do were it not clear that Romeo kills the very
image of his former self.

Romeo's sentiments toward Paris—"By heaven, I love thee better
than myself, / For I come hither arm'd against myself" (5.3.64–65)—
reiterate his earlier sentiments toward Tybalt: "I . . . love thee better
than thou canst devise." His attitude toward Paris, his antagonist in
love, is remarkable for its generosity: "O, give me thy hand, / One
writ with me in sour misfortune's book! / I'll bury thee in a triumphant grave" (5.3.81–83). He is no less generous toward Tybalt,
his antagonist in honor:

> . . . liest thou there in thy bloody sheet?
> O, what more favor can I do to thee,

Than with that hand that cut thy youth in twain
To sunder his that was thine enemy?
Forgive me, cousin!

(5.3.97–101)

Romeo's generosity underscores the distance between him and his peers, between his earlier role playing as chivalric lover and avenger, and his present self. The miserly spirit of Mercutio's repeated curse, "A plague a' both your houses!" (3.1.91–106), emphasizes the point of Romeo's capacity for compassion and forgiveness in the face of death.

We hear an echo of the early Romeo when he resorts to the "light" imagery so characteristic of his earlier descriptions of Juliet's beauty: "A grave? O no, a lanthorn, . . . / For here lies Juliet, and her beauty makes / This vault a feasting presence full of light" (5.3.84–86).[18] To focus on the imagery of Romeo's final words, though, is to ignore the emotional experience he expresses: the hushed, personal quality of utterance, the privateness, the intimacy of tone. To fashion a tragic protagonist who can speak the phrases of romantic love, Thompson notes, "one does not need to change the conventions so much as the tone of voice in which the familiar phrases are spoken" (1971, 72). Romeo's observation of graphic detail continues from his recollection of the Apothecary. This capacity for concrete description of Juliet's beauty creates the irony of his nearly discovering the truth:

O my love, my wife,
Death, that hath suck'd the honey of thy breath,
Hath had no power yet upon thy beauty:
Thou art not conquer'd, beauty's ensign yet
Is crimson in thy lips and in thy cheeks,
And death's pale flag is not advanced there.

(5.3.91–96)

Oxymora are obsolete; the paradox of Juliet's living corpse exists as a theatrical not a rhetorical reality. More significantly, Romeo is no longer capable of stock Petrarchan devices. Though richly metaphoric, his language is transformed by soberness, eroticism, and sardonic humor:

Ah, dear Juliet,
Why art thou yet so fair? Shall I believe
That unsubstantial Death is amorous,

And that the lean abhorred monster keeps
Thee here in dark to be his paramour?

(5.3.101–5)

The gulf between the protagonists' different concepts of love—the essentially comic conflict of the first two acts—narrows. Romeo breaks out of role playing as he overcomes the obstacle of romanticizing and discovers an authentic emotional commitment. Like the male protagonists of the romantic comedies, he achieves self-realization obliquely through learning how to love. Even as Hamlet dies at the moment he is fit to rule Denmark, Romeo dies at the moment he is capable of reciprocating the depth and totality of Juliet's emotional commitment. Finally worthy of Juliet, he seems capable of a mutuality of devotion with her based upon confidence, generosity, and an intimacy of expression that honestly conveys his emotions.

The gulf between the two extraordinary protagonists and their ordinary culture—the essentially tragic conflict of the last three acts—widens. Both Romeo's refusal to fight and Juliet's refusal to marry are overwhelmed by Veronese forces so powerful as to seem instinctual rather than cultural. We might be tempted to believe Shakespeare points the lesson of the fate of iconoclasts were not his protagonists so sympathetically portrayed and those who unquestioningly subscribe to Verona's dictates so shallow. In attempting to understand why Romeo and Juliet defy social convention, we come to understand not only its antagonism but its irrelevance to their lives. Because our first glimpse of each of them reveals their indifference to "honorable" street fighting and "honorable" arranged marriage, we are not surprised at their commitment—despite strong cultural tides propelling them in the opposite direction—to the supremacy of their personal relationship.

Except momentarily when Romeo decries his effeminacy and when Juliet learns of her cousin's death by her husband's hand, the two are never at odds with one another. In *Othello*, however, the male protagonist's loss of faith in the female protagonist *constitutes* the action of the tragedy. Female chastity is never an issue in *Romeo and Juliet;* it is *the* issue in *Othello*. *Romeo and Juliet* externalizes stereotypical masculine attitudes toward love and honor in various foils—Paris and Mercutio, Benvolio and Tybalt. Because the conflict is social, the tragedy retains a degree of comic sensibility. *Othello* also externalizes stereotypically masculine attitudes toward love and honor in this way but internalizes them as well. Because the conflict is psychological, within Othello's psyche, the tragedy plumbs greater depths.

3

Othello: Female Subjectivity and the Ovidian Discursive Tradition

> Possession is loss.
>
> —Dante, *La Divina Commedia*

In *Romeo and Juliet* and *Antony and Cleopatra*, the love story is held in tension with realms of action, whether feud or empire. In *Othello* the drama is built along simpler lines: military action—the threat of the Turkish attack—begins in act 1, only to conclude in act 2. The focus on the love story allows the dramatic conflict to be internalized; conflicting notions of honor and love are played out not on Verona's streets but within Othello's psyche. The peripeteia of *Romeo and Juliet* occurs when Tybalt's and Mercutio's concern with honor assaults Romeo's commitment to Juliet; the peripeteia of *Othello* occurs when Iago exploits Othello's idealized notion of honor and shatters his fragile understanding of Desdemona. Shakespeare stresses the same end by different means; that is, the innocence and inexperience of the male protagonist in heterosexual relations. Whereas he emphasizes the ennoblement of Romeo's character, however, he emphasizes the deterioration of Othello's nobility.

It is possible to view both Juliet and Desdemona as passive females suffering the consequences of male concerns from the realm of "heroic" action. There are similarities in their situations, to be sure: both male protagonists' concern with honor plays an integral part in overpowering their incipient understanding of the love the female protagonists bear them, resulting in Romeo's physical separation from Juliet and Othello's psychological estrangement from Desdemona. Even as neither female is heroic in the conventional sense of performance of deeds within public realms of action—given the constraints of the patriarchal cultures in which their plays are set—they are remarkably resilient and strong when it comes to matters of the heart. It is no accident that Shakespeare endows them with the intelligence and wit to make choices, the independence and courage to take risks, the confidence and faith to give and accept love without hesitation or qualification, and particularly in Desdemona, a constancy that is absolute and a generosity that merges into charity.

Juliet possesses the strength to choose a Montague for her husband but not to stand up to her father. Her crisis, therefore, lies in her violation of social taboo and her inability to defend herself from Capulet's accusations by revealing that violation. Desdemona possesses the strength to choose a Moor for her husband and to stand up to her father as well. Her crisis lies in Othello's loss of belief in her and her inability to defend herself successfully from his accusations. While it is possible to speculate on the effect Juliet's revelation of marriage might have on Capulet, it is impossible to speculate on the effect that such a revelation of innocence might have on Othello. The certainty of her innocence depends upon, of course, not any revelation or proof, but the strength of Othello's faith in her. Othello's demand for ocular proof to settle the matter of Desdemona's fidelity, Frank Kermode points out, "is logically absurd, since there could be no such proof of *fidelity;* evidence can only be on the other side" (1974, 1201). Had Shakespeare set out to demonstrate how necessary is mutuality of emotional commitment within a love relationship and how crucial is reciprocity of belief in one another, he could not have presented a more convincing tale than *Othello*.

The female protagonist's realistic love is foregrounded in *Romeo and Juliet* against a background that is quite diverse in character. Verona offers multiple perspectives on love and honor. The Petrarchism of Romeo and Paris, the reasonableness of Benvolio, and the Ovidian stance of Mercutio jostle for our attention and, not coincidentally, accentuate the authenticity of Juliet's love. Tybalt's and Mercutio's preoccupation with honor is juxtaposed to Benvolio's and Romeo's indifference to it. The female protagonist's plain truth and innocence is foregrounded in *Othello,* however, against a background characterized not by diversity but uniformity. In Venice and Cyprus all the male characters—Brabantio, Roderigo, Cassio, and Othello—share notions of love and honor that are drawn out, played upon, and exploited by Iago. This uniformity of perspective leads critics to observe that the play is primarily concerned with the way men talk about, feel about, and treat women (Stilling 1976, 145–65; Neely, 1977). Indeed, the central fissure or gap which *Othello* interrogates is that dividing the constructions of women held by the male characters in the play on the one hand, and Shakespeare's theatrical representation of women on the other.

Critical responses to *Othello*, like those to *Romeo and Juliet*, have been characterized by a debate between two polarized interpretations of character. Coleridge, A. C. Bradley, and their followers stress Othello's nobility and his innocence of blame.[1] They are labeled "sentimentalist" by T. S. Eliot, F. R. Leavis, and their followers, who instead emphasize Othello's tragic flaw and his responsibility for the tragic action.[2] The first approach, taken to the extreme, tends to erode characterization and reduce dramatic action to medieval allegory. Othello becomes an Everyman torn between abstractions of Good (Desdemona) and Evil (Iago). The second approach, taken to its extreme, tends to deny Othello's nobility and reduce the tragic action to that of melodrama. The critical conflict between the privileging of nobility or the privileging of tragic flaw turns on the central question: is the best about us the truth about us or is the worst about us the truth about us? Critical preoccupation with Aristotelian prescriptions about degrees of nobility and tragic flaw results in a focus on the conflict between Othello and Iago. Interpretations of Desdemona's character are subsidiary, often contingent on the views of Othello. Those who would idealize him tend to idealize her as well; those who would disparage him tend to disparage her as well. In either case the tendency is not to view her as a complex character.[3]

Comic Impulses

Winifred Nowottny's elucidation of the conflicting forces of justice and love in *Othello* shifts attention from Iago to Desdemona. Love and faithfulness cannot be "proved" by the mechanisms of justice, reason, and evidence, she maintains; indeed, Shakespeare's point is that "love is beyond reason" (1951–52, 334). When Robert Heilman distinguishes between "wit" and "witchcraft"([1956] 1967)—his metaphors for Iago's cunning reason and Desdemona's love[4]—he parallels the distinction between justice and love drawn by Nowottny. Both critics highlight the antithetical relationship between rational and irrational impulses in the play,[5] but Nowottny further suggests that Othello's only immunity against Iago and jealousy is a continuation of faith in Desdemona and her love. Marital fidelity, she points out, "is the case par excellence where the only protection of the accused is that intuitive belief in her integrity which should have precluded accusation" (1951–52, 335). Desdemona emerges in this context as the moral center of the tragedy.

The aspect of intuitive belief most insistently interrogated by the dramatic action of *Othello* is the relationship between confidence in oneself and trust in another. "Only the person who has faith in himself is able to be faithful to others," Erich Fromm maintains.

"What matters in relation to love is the faith in one's own love; in its ability to produce love in others, and in its reliability" (1956, 123–24). The opening scenes of *Othello* emphasize not only Othello's confidence in himself but his trust in Desdemona. Ease and assurance characterize his response to the threat of Brabantio's wrath:

> Let him do his spite;
> My services which I have done the signiory
> Shall out-tongue his complaints. . . .

> I must be found.
> My parts, my title, and my perfect soul
> Shall manifest me rightly. . . .

> Keep up your bright swords, for the dew will rust them. . . .

> Hold your hands,
> Both you of my inclining, and the rest.
> Were it my cue to fight, I should have known it
> Without a prompter.
>
> (1.2.17–84)

The contrast between his reputation and history as warrior, which are described, and his courtesy of manner and his spacious style of speaking, which we see and hear on stage, creates an impression of great strength and energy governed by restraint. The sense of self conveyed here culminates in his final words in the play, "I have done the state some service, and they know 't" (5.2.339), leading some critics to believe that he regains dignity before his death.

Othello's occupation as a soldier has, of necessity, acquainted him with the matter of trust in others—and, because he has risked his life time and again in battle, it is a trust that is absolute. Shakespeare would have us pity "the vulnerability of his great-hearted soldier," Robert Ornstein maintains, "who, used to absolute trust in himself and in those about him (his treasured Michael Cassio), requires certainty in love when there can be no certainty but the intuition of the heart" ([1960] 1965, 229). Accordingly, Othello's trust in Desdemona at the outset of the drama is absolute. He twice wagers his life upon her faith:

> If you do find me foul in her report,
> The trust, the office I do hold of you,
> Not only take away, but let your sentence

Even fall upon my life. . . .
My life upon her faith!

(1.3.117–294)

In *Othello,* as in *Romeo and Juliet,* Shakespeare continues to high-light hazarding, risk, and choice in love. Desdemona shares with Juliet an independence of spirit and a self-confidence that allow not only their defiance of cultural convention but their violation of cultural taboo in their choice of a Montague and a Moor for hus-bands. Because the consequences of their respective choice of hus-band constitute the dramatic action of both tragedies, it is easy to overlook the less obvious unconventionality of Juliet's proposal of marriage to Romeo and Desdemona's initiation of courtship with Othello. Othello's description of their acquaintanceship reveals that it is Desdemona who woos him:

> My story being done,
> She gave me for my pains a world of sighs;
> She swore, in faith 'twas strange, 'twas passing strange;
> 'Twas pitiful, 'twas wondrous pitiful.
> She wish'd she had not heard it; yet she wish'd
> That heaven had made her such a man. She thank'd me,
> And bade me, if I had a friend that lov'd her,
> I should teach him how to tell my story,
> And that would woo her. Upon this hint I spake. . . .

(1.3.158–66)

Whether we emphasize her "hint" in this passage or whether we emphasize instead Othello's narration of his personal history itself as an attempt to win her, their courtship is reciprocal in nature. In either case Desdemona is what Brabantio abhors, at least "half the wooer."

We may try, in the way critics itemize Iago's motives or Othello's vulnerabilities, to envision Desdemona weighing in the balance Othello's various characteristics either alone or against those of other suitors: psychological traits, physical attributes, wealth, social posi-tion, and so on. But it is a futile exercise because the only "evidence" Shakespeare offers is Othello's "She lov'd me for the dangers I had pass'd" (1.3.167) and Desdemona's "I saw Othello's visage in his mind" (1.3.252). Everything in the choice of a marital partner finally depends upon not any rational consideration of empirical criteria, but upon an irrational act, an arbitrary choice, or decision. The guarantee of a marital union relies on this decision to venture forth into the

unknown committed to the marital partner. In this consent to take
new chances, in this readiness to adapt to change, lies the foundation
of a new life.

"So opposite to marriage" was Desdemona before meeting Othello
(reminiscent of Juliet's indifference to marriage before meeting
Romeo) that she shunned the "wealthy curled darlings" of Venice.
Othello wooed an admitted prize among women, Rosalie Colie
notes; Desdemona, however, "studied her husband and chose him at
considerable expense to herself" (1974, 167). Whether or not we
agree with this speculation about Desdemona's behavior during
courtship, it is clear that she takes a great risk in choosing Othello—as
Brabantio's response to her "divided duty" speech emphasizes—and
that she takes that risk knowingly. Her declaration before the Venetian Senate reveals her understanding of the unconventionality of her
choice and intimates her willingness to face its consequent challenges:

> That I did love the Moor to live with him,
> My downright violence, and storm of fortunes,
> May trumpet to the world. My heart's subdu'd
> Even to the very quality of my lord.
>
> (1.3.248–51)

Othello emphasizes in a parallel passage not risk but an understanding of the single state he relinquishes:

> But that I love the gentle Desdemona,
> I would not my unhoused free condition
> Put into circumscription and confine
> For the sea's worth.
>
> (1.2.25–28)

His mention of his "unhoused free condition" hints at the panoramic
adventures that contribute, perhaps, to his "free and open nature."
There is much mention of spaciousness, skies, seas, and sea ventures
in the opening scenes of the play, all of which contribute to the
exoticism of his character and to delineate his adventurous past. But
his "disastrous chances" and "moving accidents" also remind us of the
venturing forth and hazarding in sexual relations that Shakespeare
uses time and again to convey the psychological state of readiness for
intimacy. Romeo expresses his love as a sea venture, suggesting luck
and skill set against natural hazards (2.2.82–84). Bassanio ventures
forth for Portia as a Jason in quest of the golden fleece:

For the four winds blow in from every coast
Renowned suitors, and her sunny locks
Hang on her temples like a golden fleece,
Which makes her seat of Belmont Colchis' strond,
And many Jasons come in quest of her.
                    (*The Merchant of Venice*, 1.1.168–72)

Clearly the relationship between Desdemona and Othello is neither
Brabantio's "maiden, never bold" bewitched by "foul charms" nor
the mere lust Iago perceives between "a super-subtle Venetian" and
"an erring barbarian." Nor is the relationship an uncontrollable
romantic passion. Although the emphasis is on Desdemona's initiative, her choice, and her risk, both she and Othello act with
considered knowledge of what they are doing.

Shakespeare alters his source, Cinthio's *Gli hecatommithi,* where
there is only the mention that Desdemona's parents opposed her
marriage ([1566] 1973, 242), when he invents Brabantio's character.
Brabantio's challenges—first to Othello, then to Desdemona—accentuate the protagonists' mutual love and trust in one another. Indeed,
both Brabantio's challenges and Iago's obscenities exist as much to
accentuate the quality of the relationship between the protagonists as
to prompt the opening action of the play. The positive impression
made upon the audience by the theatrical representation of Othello's
and Desdemona's love for one another is emphasized by the negative
impressions it cancels out—those of Brabantio and Iago. In depicting
their relationship as unrespectable only from the limited perspective
of the wronged father and as unnatural only from the limited perspective of the depraved villain, Shakespeare emphasizes the firmness of
the foundation of their reciprocal belief and trust.[6]

Romeo and Juliet mutually affirm their love for one another in the
privacy, indeed, secrecy, of the Capulet orchard; Othello and Desdemona mutually declare their love for one another in the public forum
of the Venetian Senate. In Iago's and Othello's private exchange of
vows that ends the deception scene, critics perceive a satanic inversion
of the marriage ceremony. In Desdemona's and Othello's trial before
the Senate, though, with its public exchange of vows, the audience
observes an enactment of the marriage ceremony:

Desdemona. I saw Othello's visage in his mind,
    And to his honors and his valiant parts
    Did I my soul and fortunes consecrate. . . .
Othello. My life upon her faith!

                                                    (1.3.252–94)

Their relationship is challenged not by a largely external threat such as the feud in *Romeo and Juliet* but by one internal to the relationship as well. Because Shakespeare is concerned to dramatize a loss of belief that is psychological, he emphasizes at the outset of the tragedy the strength of the foundation that is to crumble.

Yet Shakespeare does not idealize this union by blinking at its sexual aspect. He gives Desdemona, like Juliet, surprising candor:

> . . . if I be left behind,
> A moth of peace, and he go to the war,
> The rites for why I love him are bereft me,
> And I a heavy interim shall support
> By his dear absence. Let me go with him.
>
> (1.3.255–59)

Desdemona's frank mention of the "rites" of marriage, A. D. Nuttall suggests, "throws Othello off balance" (1983, 138).[7] He does not reciprocate her candid expression of sexuality:

> Let her have your voice.
> Vouch with me, heaven, I therefore beg it not
> To please the palate of my appetite,
> Nor to comply with heat (the young affects
> In me defunct) and proper satisfaction;
> But to be free and bounteous to her mind. . . .
>
> (1.3.260–65)

Instead he is concerned, perhaps because of his acute awareness of his status as an alien in Venetian society, that his accommodation of her wishes not be interpreted as sexually motivated on his part. His speech, therefore, quite deliberately inverts the emphasis of hers. If her line of thought moves from the mental to the physical—from "I saw Othello's visage in his mind" to "the rites for why I love him"—then his moves from the physical to the mental—from "the palate of my appetite" to "be free and bounteous to her mind."

Although the sea voyages of Desdemona and Othello to Cyprus have a military rationale in the action of the play, they symbolize as well the protagonists' joint venturing forth into the state of marriage, echoing the many verbal references to quests, sea ventures, and hazarding in love throughout the romantic comedies. Shakespeare's de-emphasis on the military action in act 2 coincides with his use of the voyages in this way. In *Romeo and Juliet*, the Ovidian strain voiced by Mercutio, as we have seen, plays a role secondary to the Petrarchan strain voiced by the protagonist. In *Othello*, Cassio's

idealizing courtly discourse plays a role secondary to Iago's misogyny. Cassio's hyperboles on Desdemona resolve into hyperboles
describing the dangers husband and wife pass and their safe arrivals,
one following the other, at Cyprus. He publicly emblazons their
reunion in the manner of an epithalamium: may Othello "bless this
bay with his tall ship" and "Make love's quick pants in Desdemona's
arms" (2.1.79–80).

The device of the lovers' separate arrivals at Cyprus creates the
emotional complexity and richness of the scene. It allows in their
greeting of one another both an enactment of their original meeting—
which the audience never sees—and a dramatic reinforcement of the
impression made by their earlier narrations and declarations before
the Venetian Senate. Othello's happiness at Desdemona's safety therefore expresses his original sense of fulfillment matched by disbelief:
"O my fair warrior! . . . / It gives me wonder great as my content /
To see you here before me. O my soul's joy!" (2.1.182–84). Together
with "She lov'd me for the dangers I had pass'd," this is our first
glimpse of the emotional condition of the man whose life has been
one of solitude and whose self-knowledge, consequently, derives
from the arena of military action rather than the realm of intimate
relationships. Othello's tragedy consists in the fact that he leaves the
battlefield, if we agree with Nuttall in this connection, and enters a
world for which he is not fit: "*Othello* is the story of a hero who
went into a house" (1983, 134). The theatrical enactment of the lovers'
reunion is expressive of emotions of both greeting one another after
separation and meeting one another for the first time; it serves as a
symbolic union as well. It is, therefore, their moment of greatest
felicity.

Yet Othello's happiness at his discovery of Desdemona at such a late
time in life is haunted by fear of loss. With any hope he may have had
for a romantic partner perhaps faded, the fulfillment she brings him is
so total it seems to him almost more than he deserves:

>   If it were now to die,
> 'Twere now to be most happy; for I fear
> My soul hath her content so absolute
> That not another comfort like to this
> Succeeds in unknown fate.

                                                        (2.1.189–93)

His sense of absoluteness in love here, as later—"when I love thee
not, / Chaos is come again" (3.3.91–92)—is rooted in his inexperience in love. It suggests, like the active imagination and the need

for certainty he soon reveals, the tone of Donne's *Songs and Sonnets*. Desdemona's understanding of love as a dynamic force is more optimistic: "The heavens forbid / But that our loves and comforts should increase, / Even as our days do grow!" (2.1.193–95). In her calmer acceptance of the permutations of love and the mutability of life, she echoes the speaker in Shakespeare's sonnets.[8] Her understanding of love's "quotidian joys," to quote Carol Thomas Neely (1977, 138)—its flow and ebb with the pattern of daily existence, its changing process of increase and decrease—is an attitude complementary to Othello's. Given time—time granted lovers in Shakespearean comedy and romance—her love might have the healing power to assuage his fears. The mood at this moment is a very much like that of the conclusions of the comedies, full of the hope and promise of "the two become one" in marriage, of the woman who chooses and risks in choosing, of the man who is fulfilled beyond belief at her having chosen him.

Patriarchy, Misogyny, Honor

The state of marriage in Shakespeare is not merely a cultural construct; it is a dramatic context within which either comic or tragic forces may appear and play themselves out, dominate, or disappear. It can provide an opportunity for Desdemona's belief in Othello to help him achieve self-knowledge through learning how to love, but it can provide a context for Iago's manipulation of him as well. In distinguishing between education and manipulation, Fromm observes that education depends upon belief in the growth of potentialities, as is suggested by its Latin root, *educere*—"to lead forth, to bring out that which is potentially present" (1956, 124 n.3). Manipulation, its opposite, depends instead upon a belief in power. In a precise inversion of the educational process, Iago "leads forth" and "brings out" Othello's insecurities and doubts. "To believe in power that exists is identical with disbelief in the growth of potentialities which are as yet unrealized," Fromm points out. "There is no rational faith in power. There is submission to it or, on the part of those who have it, the wish to keep it. While to many power seems to be the most real of all things, the history of man has proved it to be the most unstable of all human achievements" (1956, 125–26). The mutual exclusivity of the impulses of belief and manipulation, love and power, provides a context for understanding villainy in Shakespeare. He sees the archenemies of order, Ornstein maintains, as individualists "who cast off all bonds of blood or affection—who hunger for power because they cannot love" (1972, 222).

Because in *Romeo and Juliet* male competition manifests itself in the violence of the feud, sexual issues surface only lightheartedly and briefly in the Capulet and Montague servants' banter and in Mercutio's Ovidian discourse. Because in *Othello* the action is streamlined of similar external violence and focused upon the love story, male competition manifests itself instead in what Coppélia Kahn perceives as "an interlocking chain of sexual offenses and revenges that makes each of [the men] either cuckold, cuckolder, or both, each one in sexual competition with another" (1981, 143). To observe that the action of the play is focused upon the love story is not to deny that the issues raised in the Desdemona–Othello relationship are anticipated or reiterated like concentric circles expanding from the center in the peripheral relationships between Bianca and Cassio and Emilia and Iago. But it is Desdemona who is linked in several relationships, real or imagined, to every man in the drama—Brabantio, Othello, Roderigo, Cassio, even Iago: "Now I do love her too, / . . . to diet my revenge" (2.1.291–94).

We might be more inclined to agree with Kahn's view were not Iago Shakespeare's consummate manipulator—any "interlocking chain" is one of his creation. All of the "sexual offenses and revenges" in the play are those fabricated by him, the stuff of either his "motive-hunting" or his manipulation of each of the male characters. Yet for all his need to invent, his task is simplified because it depends for its success upon exploiting existing attitudes: a tendency to both idealize and devalue women and a preoccupation with female chastity and male honor. Rather than a satanic figure responsible for terrible deeds such as murder, or a sinister machiavel with a grandiose motive for furthering himself in the world, petty malice and petty hustling characterize Iago at the outset of the play. Rather than a simple incarnation of evil duping all the other characters on stage, he is quite human in his ability to tell people exactly what they want to hear. The plausibility of his "honesty" depends upon his forthrightness and frankness in expressing his likes and dislikes in people.

In public, Iago's jokes about women, such as those in the exchange with Desdemona on the quay, do not cross the line that separates respectability and obscenity. In private, however, they express his hatred of his wife and all women. Women exist not to love but to satisfy men's physical appetites; female sexuality is insatiable. It is impossible to differentiate the premise from the conclusion within the circular logic of this credo, although his gulling of Roderigo depends for its success upon the notion of female insatiability:

> It cannot be long that Desdemona should continue her love to the Moor. . . . She must change for youth; when she is sated with his body, she will find the error of her choice. She must have change, she must. . . .
> (1.3.341–52)

Her eye must be fed; and what delight shall she have to look on the devil?
When the blood is made dull with the act of sport, there should be, again
to inflame it and to give satiety a fresh appetite, loveliness in favor,
sympathy in years, manners, and beauties—all which the Moor is defec-
tive in. Now, for want of these requir'd conveniences, her delicate tender-
ness will find itself abus'd, begin to heave the gorge, disrelish and abhor
the Moor; very nature will instruct her in it and compel her to some
second choice.

(2.1.225–35)

His gulling of Othello similarly depends upon the notion of female
insatiability, but must not prima facie sound disgusting:

Ay, there's the point; as (to be bold with you)
Not to affect many proposed matches
Of her own clime, complexion, and degree,
Whereto we see in all things nature tends—
Foh, one may smell in such, a will most rank,
Foul disporpotions, thoughts unnatural.
But (pardon me) I do not in position
Distinctly speak of her, though I may fear
Her will, recoiling to her better judgement,
May fall to match you with her country forms,
And happily repent.

(3.3.228–38)

His technique of insinuation suffices because Othello's febrile, lively,
active imagination requires no more than suggestion to feed it.

Not a paucity but a plethora of motives in Iago's first soliloquy
prompts Coleridge's famous description of it as "the motive-hunting
of motiveless malignity" ([1960] 1963, 1:206). Nuttall more recently
notes that Iago "chooses which emotions he will experience. He is
not just motivated, like other people. Instead he *decides* to be motivated" (1983, 142–43). Iago does decide to act as though the rumor
that Othello is familiar with Emilia were true: "I hate the Moor; /
And it is thought abroad that 'twixt my sheets / H 'as done my office"
(1.3.385–87). His use of the coordinating conjunction "and" rather
than the adverbial subordinator "because," however, exposes his
rationale as a non sequitur. He is, of course, incapable of jealousy for
a wife he hates, but that does not prevent his cynical appropriation of
jealousy as a convenient motive that suffices just as well as all the
other motives: "I do suspect the lusty Moor / Hath leap'd into my
seat" (2.1.295–96). The point is that while Iago is incapable of either
love or jealousy, Othello is deeply capable of both.

The first link in the chain of male competition over Desdemona is Iago's exploitation of Brabantio's status as father: "Look to your house, your daughter, and your bags!" (1.1.80). The reference to Desdemona as chattel—suggestive of Kant's second imperative in its deprivation of human dignity—is but the first of many of its kind in the play. For Brabantio, unlike Leonato in *Much Ado*, emotional pain at the loss of his daughter overrides concern with reputation. Shakespeare exploits not his but Cassio's concern with reputation as a parallel to Othello's concern with honor. Fathers of brides in both comedy and tragedy, however, have in common with one another, and with Iago, the language of possession:

Leonato. But mine, and mine I lov'd, and mine I prais'd,
    And mine that I was proud on, mine so much
    That I myself was to myself not mine,
    Valuing of her. . . .
                                          (*Much Ado*, 4.1.136–39)

Brabantio.   . . . how got she out?
. . . .
    O thou foul thief, where hast thou stow'd my daughter?
. . . .
    She is . . . stol'n from me.
                          (*Othello*, 1.1.169; 1.2.62; 1.3.60)

In this way Shakespeare anticipates and elucidates Othello's concern with possession in response to the "loss" of his wife: "I had rather be a toad / And live upon the vapor of a dungeon / Than keep a corner in the thing I love / For others' uses" (3.3.270–73). The first representation of jealousy in the play is not Othello's but Brabantio's; the husband's sexual jealousy in act 3 merely follows and parallels the father's sexual jealousy in act 1.

Our impression of *Othello* as a play concerned with men's treatment of women begins when a father, publicly humiliated by his daughter, first lies about her attraction to her husband and then calls her whore. Confronting a daughter's love for another man is bound to be an emotionally difficult experience for a father. If she marries a man of his choosing, the formal ritual of giving her away in marriage mitigates the pain of her loss; but if she elopes with a man of her own choosing, any formalized, ritualized expression of possessiveness is denied him and sexual jealousy itself surfaces. Brabantio initially denies the emotional pain of Desdemona's responsibility in the elopement by accusing Othello of using "chains of magic," "foul charms," "drugs," and "minerals" to beguile her away from him. Confronted with her complete honesty about her "divided duty," he finds emotional relief in thinking his daughter is a whore, "Look to her, Moor, if thou hast eyes to see; / She has deceiv'd her father, and may thee" (1.3.292–93), just as Othello finds emotional relief in thinking his wife is a whore: "she must die, else she'll betray more men" (5.2.6). If Iago's acumen enables him to exploit the vulnerability of possession inherent in Brabantio's paternal role, then Brabantio's jealousy, in turn, causes him to exploit the vulnerability of possession inherent in Othello's new marital role. In so doing Brabantio enables Iago to reiterate his words to Othello in the deception scene: "Look to your wife, observe her well with Cassio, / . . . She did deceive her father, marrying you" (3.3.197–206).

Both father and husband construct daughter and wife as whore with remarkable ease when they discover, or seem to discover, her love of another man. Neither man is capable of understanding Desdemona's subjectivity; that is, comprehending in her a humanity that overrides her relationship to either of them. To both father and husband the loss of daughter and wife, real or imagined, is focused upon her loss of chastity. "Are they married?" (1.1.167) is Brabantio's immediate inquiry; "O curse of marriage, / That we can call these delicate creatures ours, / And not their appetites!" (3.3.268–70) is Othello's lament. Although the incest taboo prevents paternal-filial sexual interaction, the institution of patriarchal marriage grants the father control of the daughter's sexuality until marriage when it becomes the possession and the responsibility of the husband. A man's trustworthiness in worldly matters is called into question if it is known that he cannot manage his own household, that is, control the sexuality of a daughter or a wife.

The construct of marriage as a male-centered institution—one that is concerned with male control of female sexuality and the female procreative process, or, as anthropologist Gayle Rubin puts it, "the traffic in women" (1975)—has been with us since the origin of patriarchal cultures. The etymologies of the words *marriage* and *marry* reveal that their Latin roots, *maritus* and *mas*, denote "husband, man, male."[9] A woman brings her chastity to marriage; she gives this to a man; he possesses her and her virtue. Yet a husband is curiously dependent upon that chastity. "Men have property in women," as Keith Thomas puts it; "the value of this property," however, "is immeasurably diminished if the woman at any time has sexual relations with anyone other than her husband" (1959, 210). A husband's possession of a wife and her chastity is a possession that is particularly fraught with anxiety since fidelity cannot be proven and infidelity does not necessarily produce evidence. Because the institution of patriarchal marriage makes a husband's honor depend upon his wife's chastity, men in *Othello* are concerned with honor in a way that women are not.

The double standard dictates that men may "sow wild oats" while women may not, requiring women different in kind from those men marry. If a husband strays, he confirms both his own potency and his power over other men by exposing their inability to control the female sexuality under their guardianship. If a wife strays, however, she calls attention to her husband's impotence and his inability to control her: "though the husband may be said to 'own' his wife's sexual favors, while under the double standard she has no exclusive claim to his, he is under a certain obligation to keep her sexually satisfied. If she remains faithful, she in effect certifies his virility; if she strays, she calls it into question" (Kahn 1981, 121). Sexual jealousy is concerned not with one's own lack of satisfaction, but with the lack of satisfaction of one's partner—with the suspicion or the fear that one does not sexually satisfy another. Othello's expressions of jealousy focus not on love but sexuality; his concern is not the nature of Desdemona's affection for Cassio but her sexual favors to him. His jealousy seems base because it is limited in its concern to the sexual. Such a narrow focus on this singular aspect of Desdemona both denies her complexity and diminishes her humanity. As Colie suggests, Othello "ceases to see Desdemona whole: as she loses her integrity for him, he sees her only in parts" (1974, 100).

Jealousy does offer emotional satisfaction—"I am abus'd, and my relief / Must be to loathe her" (3.3.267–68)—the emotional relief of the expression of self-pity, self-righteousness, and revenge.

> No longer the sole possessor of his wife's sexuality, the cuckold knows what he is well enough: mocked with horns for his deficient virility, deprived of honor, the butt of ridicule, he is unmanned, a monster. But some redress is open to him, though even revenge will never take away the stigma of his horns; he can unwoman his wife by calling her whore, a stigma *she* will find it hard to live down. (Kahn 1981, 145)

Indeed, the retaliatory reciprocal exchange of "whore" for "cuckold" is a twisted perversion of the mutual exchange of belief and trust in one another that forms the foundation upon which an intimate relationship is built. It is also the natural culmination of excessive concern with honor and chastity. In endowing Desdemona with absolute purity and innocence and in emphasizing these traits, Shakespeare holds up for examination the adequacy of chastity as the single standard by which to measure female value. Her chastity, absolute though it is, means not a jot in saving her life. Because male honor depends in part upon female chastity, Shakespeare also calls into question the adequacy of honor as the single standard by which to measure male value. Neilson and Hill make the point that Othello's natural goodness, "the native honor which makes duplicity as alien to him as cowardice," becomes a weakness for Iago to play upon (1942, 1094); others, such as Council (1973) and Klene (1975), claim that it is not jealousy but concern with reputation and honor that causes Othello's tragedy.

By portraying Cassio's response to his loss of reputation, Shakespeare anticipates and elucidates Othello's response to his loss of honor. Iago exploits and manipulates the military ideals of both soldiers. He feigns concern with one's "good name":

> Good name in man and woman, dear my lord,
> Is the immediate jewel of their souls.
> Who steals my purse steals trash; 'tis something, nothing;
> 'Twas mine, 'tis his, and has been slave to thousands;
> But he that filches from me my good name
> Robs me of that which not enriches him,
> And makes me poor indeed.
>
> (3.3.155–61)

Iago's feigned concern with one's "good name" precisely matches Othello's genuine concern with "estimation" and Cassio's with "reputation":

> *Othello.*   . . . when light-wing'd toys
>   Of feather'd Cupid seel with wanton dullness
>   My speculative and offic'd instruments,
>   That my disports corrupt and taint my business,
>   Let housewives make a skillet of my helm,
>   And all indign and base adversities
>   Make head against my estimation!
>
> (1.3.268–74)

> *Cassio.* Reputation, reputation, reputation! O, I have lost my reputation! I have lost the immortal part of myself, and what remains is bestial. My reputation, Iago, my reputation!
>
> (2.3.262–65)

Too, Iago requires a particular mentality on the part of his victim: Cassio is a lightweight, a soldier capable of drinking on duty. He is, furthermore, a man whose shame at his dishonorable conduct is so great that he is incapable of speaking to Othello on his own behalf.

Othello's identity is inextricably bound up in his military role; his status in Venetian society depends upon his worthiness as a hired mercenary. Desdemona's apparent adultery calls into question, therefore, not only his virility and his ability to control her, but his valuation of self as soldier and human being. It is not surprising, then, that his elegy to lost love should take the shape of an elegy to "glorious war" and the occupation of the warrior hero:

> O, now, for ever
> Farewell the tranquil mind! farewell content!
> Farewell the plumed troops and the big wars
> That make ambition virtue! O, farewell!
> Farewell the neighing steed and the shrill trump,
> The spirit-stirring drum, th' ear-piercing fife,
> The royal banner, and all quality,
> Pride, pomp, and circumstance of glorious war!
> And, O you mortal engines, whose rude throats
> Th' immortal Jove's dread clamors counterfeit,
> Farewell! Othello's occupation gone.
>
> (3.3.347–57)

Or, more to the point is Verdi's opera, "*Otello fu*"—*Othello gone*. Notions of glory, honor, gallantry, and sacrifice give Othello, like all soldiers, something to live and die for. They are the abstract concepts that necessarily shroud the reality of military existence—soldiers are the only group of humans with the license to kill. Everyone lives with the threat of dying; only soldiers live with the duty to kill. Because they relieve civilized society of the responsibility of war, it grants them the autonomy of a separate subculture when they live and venerates them as heroes when they die. It glorifies soldiers as heroes not only for performing the work of slaying others but also for offering themselves up to be slain.[10]

Control is essential to survival in the military: control allows teamwork; loss of control results in panic. Because war is primarily concerned with disintegrating the network of ties among human beings, soldiers' trust in their superiors and their loyalty to one another is crucial. Officers must command competently or troops die. Iago depends upon and exploits both Cassio's and Othello's concern with honor, but again, he requires a unique mentality on the part of his victim—Othello must be in control, must be in command. He cannot stand doubt:

> Think'st thou I' ld make a life of jealousy?
> To follow still the changes of the moon

With fresh suspicions? No! to be once in doubt
Is once to be resolv'd.

                                                              (3.3.177–80)

Othello is Hamlet's opposite. As a soldier, he cannot tolerate the state
of ambiguity. His inclination to take immediate, decisive action leads
to the paradoxical solution of *proving doubt to be true, regardless of
the truth:* "Villain, be sure thou prove my love a whore; / Be sure of
it. Give me the ocular proof" (3.3.359–60). His suspension between
two contradictory truths—"I think my wife be honest, and think she
is not" (3.3.384)—creates a condition of unbearable psychological
tension. His solution, of proving doubt to be true, is an attempt on
his part to alleviate this unbearable tension: "I'll see before I doubt;
when I doubt, prove; / And on the proof, there is no more but this,—
/ Away at once with love or jealousy!" (3.3.190–92). Yet, as Nowottny points out, any attempt such as this is futile in determining the
truth. Shakespeare "adverts to the irony at the root of all these
ironies: it is useless for Othello to say 'I'll see before I doubt; when I
doubt, prove,' since infidelity does not necessarily produce evidence
of itself and fidelity cannot be put to the proof" (1951–52, 332).
Desdemona is doomed once Othello's need for "ocular proof" forces
an equation in his mind and theatrically on stage between the tangible
and the intangible, between the handkerchief and her chastity. To
Othello, her loss of the one is synonymous with her loss of the other.
His need for certainty, his propensity for decisive action, and his
dependency upon material "proof" eventually overpower Iago's
"motiveless malignity." The thought of murder is not Iago's, but
Othello's: "How shall I murther him [Cassio], Iago? . . . I would
have him nine years a-killing. . . . Ay, let her [Desdemona] rot, and
perish, and be damn'd to-night, for she shall not live. . . . I will chop
her into messes. . . . Get me some poison, Iago, this night" (4.1.170–
204). Thus "reasonable" Iago plots himself into a corner and loses
control. In the end, he is forced beyond his original goal; his actions
are finally incommensurate with his initial intent of merely making
Othello miserable.

Othello's need for certainty is related to his need for absolutes in
love:

But I do love thee! and when I love thee not,
Chaos is come again.

                                                              (3.3.91–92)

. . . there, where I have garner'd up my heart,
Where either I must live or bear no life;

The fountain from the which my current runs
Or else dries up. . . .

(4.2.57–60)

His needs for certainty and absolutes overlap with his need to idealize
both Cassio and Desdemona. Disillusionment about Cassio, whom
he idealizes, prepares him, in a way, for disillusionment about Desdemona; disillusionment about her, whom he idealizes above all, leads
to total disillusionment about all humankind, reminding us that no
greater cynic exists than the shattered idealist. The uncertainty that
Othello cannot tolerate is, at bottom, his awareness of the inability to
know another absolutely. Human intercourse, as E. M. Forster observes somewhat pessimistically, is haunted by a spectre. Humans
cannot understand one another "except in a rough and ready way," he
maintains. We cannot reveal ourselves, even when we want to; "what
we call intimacy is only a makeshift; perfect knowledge is an illusion"
([1927] 1985, 63). Othello's illusion of his "perfect knowledge" of
Desdemona—a knowledge he attempts to secure through possessing
her—is broken when his idealized construction of her shatters, making him again aware of his original condition of isolation. The relationship between his need for certainty, absolutes, and idealization is
clear when we understand his military experience and his inexperience in love as their common source.

After such a thorough commentary on the inadequacy of frag-
mented, partial views of humanity, whether female chastity or male
honor, Othello's desire to be thought of as "an honorable murderer, if
you will; / For nought I did in hate, but all in honor" (5.2.294–95)
underscores the attenuated nature of any change in him. Heilman
comments on the irony of perceiving oneself as a murderer who is yet
honorable:

> Othello does say "murderer," and it is possible that combining "honour-
> able" with "murderer" may be a bitter irony at his own expense. But the
> second line . . . makes it very likely that he means, not "nothing but a
> murderer, trying to look honorable," but "though, alas, a murderer, still
> an honorable man." (1956, 164)

Heilman's analysis of the dual, reciprocal aspects of honor emphasizes
the distinction between the active and the passive, suggesting
Othello's deficiency in one half of the equation: "by 'honor' he means
less the 'active honor' that implies obligation of self to others than the
'passive honor' that asserts the obligation of others to oneself and
one's accompanying privilege of imposing penalties on those who

fail" (1956, 164). Honor and love would seem to be equally complex concepts, reciprocal in nature, dependent upon an exchange of different opposing capacities—giving and receiving, altruism and selfishness, generosity and expectation.

Othello's capacity for the active aspect of the exchange—giving, altruism, and generosity—is as limited in love as in honor. The constant quest for assurance means less, perhaps, "a free giving of self," than, as Heilman puts it, "a taking for self" (1956, 168). Othello's limited capacity for giving is understandable, however, because we have understood from the beginning that his love for Desdemona is a response to and is dependent upon her love for him: "She lov'd me for the dangers I had pass'd, / And I lov'd her that she did pity them" (1.3.167–68). Othello voices his insecurities and fears about the realm of intimate relations: "Haply, for I am black, / And have not those soft parts of conversation / That chamberers have, or for I am declin'd / Into the vale of years" (3.3.263–66). And he attempts to use military values to guide him through this new terrain. These insecurities, fears, and attempts, while they enable him to experience "the first miracle of love, the thing given without claim," to quote Heilman, also serve to cut him off from "the greater miracle, the transformation of self into a giver" ([1956] 1967, 341; 1956, 227).

The Female Perspective

Shakespeare represents in *Othello* the subjectivity of women in high contrast to the objectifications of them by men. Iago's false portrayal of Desdemona comes closest to crumbling when confronted by her plain truth. Her entry into the deception scene breaks—albeit momentarily—his hold over Othello's imagination: "Look where she comes: / If she be false, O then heaven mocks itself! / I'll not believe 't" (3.3.277–79). It is no coincidence, of course, that Shakespeare has the "phantasmagoric questioning, raving, mocking debate go on among the men about their stereotype women," to quote Stilling, while at the center of it Desdemona stands, a denial of "a whole tradition of masculine invention and myth" (1976, 159). This disparity, fissure, or gap between male delusion and female theatrical subjectivity is, in fact, what the dramatic action most insistently interrogates.

Male fantasies prevail in act 3; they stand the test of reality in act 4. Were Shakespeare's focus merely on the male point of view which culminates in the deception scene, he would depict women solely as they are valued by men. But his focus on the female point of view which culminates in the willow song scene places a value on women's affections that is independent from their worth in men's eyes. The female characters in *Othello* differ in this way from the female protagonist of *Troilus and Cressida*. Women in the play embody an emotional commitment the men would seem to be incapable of reciprocating. Their attitudes and feelings toward the men in their lives, moreover, sharpen the focus on male treatment of women: Desdemona's absolute devotion to Othello accentuates his cruel treatment of her; Bianca's genuine affection for Cassio highlights his ridicule of her; Emilia's obedience to Iago likewise underscores his hatred of her and all women.

Even as the story of women tutoring men in *Love's Labor's Lost* anticipates the dynamics of the love relationship in *Romeo and Juliet*, that of the true woman falsely accused in *Much Ado* anticipates the action of *Othello*. It is a story that may have fascinated Shakespeare, for he returns to it time and again throughout his career, exploring its different generic implications in plays as dissimilar as *Much Ado*, *Othello*, *Cymbeline*, and *The Winter's Tale*. In comedy, Hero is pelted with the accusations of Leonato and Claudio at the wedding altar; in tragedy, however, Desdemona confronts father and husband in separate crises. And, of course, Beatrice's justifiable anger at the humiliation of the accusation is replaced by that of Emilia. But the female protagonist is dead, not to be resurrected.

Desdemona, like Juliet, enjoys her father's love while she is a compliant, obedient daughter. Each female protagonist confronts genuine paternal anger rather than the mere prerogatives of paternal authority of the comedies, however, when she attempts to exercise her will in the choice of a marital partner. The one act Juliet is incapable of—standing up to her father and revealing the secrecy of her marriage—Desdemona disposes of as soon as she walks on stage. Yet Desdemona does not stand up to Brabantio in the sense of challenging him so much as she compassionately and pointedly answers his question. She is honest with him in the same way that Cordelia is honest with Lear. The strength and honesty of her response to her father's challenge, in fact, link her more closely to Cordelia than to Juliet. Juliet faces the threat of banishment from her father's house; Desdemona and Cordelia face the reality of paternal banishment from house and kingdom.

Desdemona and Cordelia confront situations that, although different in dramatic context, are similar in emotional content. In facing specific challenges, they dramatize the problem inherent in the female condition in a patriarchal society, a daughter's "duty" to her father when it must, upon her maturity, be "divided" with a wife's "duty" to her husband. Cordelia's response to Lear's question, "Which of you shall we say doth love us most. . . ?" (*King Lear*, 1.1.51), condemns her in her father's eyes, of course, because of her plainness on her "bond." But what are we to make of the fact that Desdemona's response to Brabantio's question, "Do you perceive in all this noble company / Where most you owe obedience?" (1.3.179–80), also condemns her, despite her eloquence on her "divided duty"? The problem is neither filial inability to adapt to the new situation nor unwillingness to split emotional commitment, but rather, paternal refusal to relinquish full share of filial attention and commitment. Lear responds to Cordelia with wounded love; Brabantio responds to Desdemona with sexual jealousy.

Desdemona skillfully manages the balancing act of acknowledging her bond to Brabantio, diplomatically elaborating upon what he needs to hear—and what she genuinely feels—before insisting on the implications of her new status as Othello's wife:

> My noble father,
> I do perceive here a divided duty:
> To you I am bound for life and education;
> My life and education both do learn me
> How to respect you; you are the lord of duty;
> I am hitherto your daughter.

                                                                        (1.3.180–85)

Desdemona understands the cyclical nature of human existence as one generation repeating the life events of another in patterns of birth, growth, marriage, maturity, and death. This understanding—one that she reiterates when she greets her husband at Cyprus—would seem to guarantee the success of her plea to her father:

> But here's my husband;
> And so much duty as my mother show'd
> To you, preferring you before her father,
> So much I challenge that I may profess
> Due to the Moor, my lord.

                                                                        (1.3.185–89)

Her analogy of her situation to that of her mother attempts to gain understanding from Brabantio by drawing him out of his present paternal role and reminding him of his past marital role in his wife's similar dilemma. Her eloquence echoes that of Isabella in *Measure for Measure;* her insistence that would-be judge project himself into the situation of offender reminds us of the comic female protagonist's persuasive appeal for empathy in pleading with Angelo for the life of her brother:

If he had been as you, and you as he,
You would have slipp'd like him. . . .
                    Go to your bosom,
Knock there, and ask your heart what it doth know
That's like my brother's fault.

(Measure for Measure, 2.2.64–138)

What emerges from this exchange is an understanding that Desdemona's self-defense depends upon her immediate comprehension, even anticipation, of Brabantio's challenge. Her confidence and resilience are based upon her new connection to Othello in her new status as partner in the joint enterprise of marriage. Taking the risk of marrying him is an active choice whose consequences she is capable of anticipating and willing to accept: "That I did love the Moor to live with him, / My downright violence, and storm of fortunes, / May trumpet to the world" (1.3.247–49). The possessiveness of her husband follows as naturally as that of her father from the premise of patriarchal marriage that operates so powerfully in this play. Yet it is difficult to understand the woman who is capable of standing up to her father, but not her husband.[11]

Desdemona is, of course, unaware of the change in Othello when she declares to Emilia, immediately following the deception scene, that "my noble Moor / Is true of mind, and made of no such baseness / As jealous creatures are. . . . / I think the sun where he was born / Drew all such humors from him" (3.4.26–31). Only in the brothel scene, when his explicit epithets "strumpet" and "whore" flay at her consciousness, does understanding dimly set in. Then so great is the shock of comprehension that her near-catatonia reminds us of Hero's swoon at the wedding altar in *Much Ado:*

Emilia. How do you, madam? how do you, my good lady?
Desdemona. Faith, half asleep.
Emilia. Good madam, what's the matter with my lord?
Desdemona. With who?
Emilia. Why, with my lord, madam.
Desdemona. Who is thy lord?
Emilia.   He that is yours, sweet lady.
Desdemona. I have none.

(4.2.96–102)

It is only in this context, I think, that we are able to make sense out of
Bradley's outrageous comparison of the suffering of Desdemona to
that of "the most loving of dumb creatures" ([1904] 1955, 147). She is
dazed, Garner more recently notes; "her mind simply cannot take in
what it encounters" (1976, 248). The source of Desdemona's loss of
confidence and resilience is, of course, the severance of her connection to Othello. She is quite aware of a loss that is no less than the loss
of her marital partner: "I have none"; that is to say, "I have no lord."
Because Othello's history is that of a warrior, as Nuttall reminds us,
the state of marriage, even before he succumbs to Iago's influence, is
disorienting to him (1983, 139). Conversely, because marriage is
Desdemona's sole adventure in life, its disintegration is disorienting to
her. That marriage depends for its existence upon a mutuality of
feeling of the kind dramatized by both protagonists throughout act 1.
Despite the constancy of her faith in Othello, the foundation of their
relationship is fissured from his loss of faith in her.

Shakespeare understands women such as Mariana in *Measure for
Measure* whose internalization of patriarchal ideals makes her vulnerable to exploitation by men such as Angelo. But he does not depict
Desdemona in this way. Melancholy though she feels, observes Harbage, "she is dauntless in defense of her love and her ideals" (1963,
366). When Othello strikes her, she stoutly responds, "I have not
deserv'd this" (4.1.241). She resolutely defends herself, in fact, from
the moment she comprehends his accusations in the brothel scene
until the moment she dies:

> *Othello.* Impudent strumpet!
> *Desdemona.*   By heaven, you do me wrong.
> *Othello.* Are not you a strumpet?
> *Desdemona.*   No, as I am a Christian.
>   If to preserve this vessel for my lord
>   From any other foul unlawful touch
>   Be not to be a strumpet, I am none.
> *Othello.* What, not a whore?
> *Desdemona.*   No, as I shall be sav'd.
>
>   (4.2.81–86)

> *Othello.* That handkerchief which I so lov'd, and gave thee,
>   Thou gav'st to Cassio.
> *Desdemona.*   No, by my life and soul!
>   Send for the man, and ask him. . . .
>   I never did
>   Offend you in my life; never lov'd Cassio

But with such general warranty of heaven
As I might love. I never gave him token.

(5.2.48–61)

Regardless of her intermittent self-defense and loss of confidence, Desdemona's devotion to Othello is unchanging. Indeed, her "active effort to mend and renew the relationship," to quote Neely, is constant (1977, 147). The closing couplet of the willow song scene quintessentially expresses her optimism concerning reconciliation and healing: "God me such uses send, / Not to pick bad from bad, but by bad mend" (4.3.104–5).

Desdemona's expectations of Brabantio's possessiveness and her ease in responding to it establish her skill in anticipating situations and her resilience in responding to them. While Brabantio's challenge demands of Desdemona simple responsibility for the consequences of her action—her choice of husband—nothing of the kind can possibly suffice in responding to Othello's accusations. Her various suspicions about the reasons for the change in him reveal a sensibility that is keenly aware of the emotional nuances and dissonances of which human ties are woven—a sensibility that is, moreover, occupied with the work of restoring those ties. First, she suspects the magic spell of the sibyl's handkerchief: "I nev'r saw this before. / Sure, there's some wonder in this handkerchief; / I am most unhappy in the loss of it" (3.4.100–2). Next, she guesses at a political matter as the cause for the change in Othello: "Something sure of state, / Either from Venice, or some unhatch'd practice / Made demonstrable here in Cyprus to him, / Hath puddled his clear spirit" (3.4.140–43). Finally, she speculates that Brabantio is the reason: "If happily you my father do suspect / An instrument of this your calling back, / Lay not your blame on me" (4.2.44–46). But Desdemona is wrong, of course, on all counts. The variety of her suspicions only accentuates the futility of any anticipation and responsibility for the consequences of her actions in her new situation.

There can be no anticipation of such a loss of faith as Othello's because it is rooted not in empirical reality, but in the mind, as Emilia understands: jealous souls "are not ever jealous for the cause, / But jealous for they're jealous. It is a monster / Begot upon itself, born on itself" (3.4.160–62). Nor can there be any defense against such a loss of faith other than a simple reaffirmation of faith. The imperatives of reason and justice are irrelevant to the realm of love and jealousy. Immunity from jealousy lies in the continuance of this act of faith, Nowottny maintains. Shakespeare "deliberately forces upon the audience the question, In what strength could Othello reject Iago? The answer would seem to be, By an affirmation of faith which is beyond reason, by the act of choosing to believe in Desdemona" (1951–52, 334).

The tragic action follows from Othello's inability to reaffirm his faith in Desdemona in this way. But it is precisely a reaffirmation of faith such as Nowottny describes that characterizes the generosity of Desdemona's response to the change in him: "I was (unhandsome warrior as I am) / Arraigning his unkindness with my soul; / But now I find I had suborn'd the witness, / And he's indicted falsely" (3.4.151–54). Desdemona kneels alone in an enactment of her reaffirmation of faith in Othello: "Unkindness may do much, / And his unkindness may defeat my life, / But never taint my love" (4.2.159–61). This visual emblem is a powerful reminder of her declaration of wedding-like vows before the Venetian Senate in act 1: "I saw Othello's visage in his mind, / And to his honors and his valiant parts / Did I my soul and fortunes consecrate" (1.3.252–54). But it also throws into high relief the inversion of the wedding ceremony in act 3—Othello kneeling side by side with Iago in an enactment of his loss of faith in her. The effect of these two stage emblems is to emphasize that his spirit erodes, while hers does not.

Desdemona's love for Othello, Nowottny concludes, is "made 'unreasonable' in a way which permits discussion of it in the drama" (1951–52, 334). The irony of Desdemona's continued obedience and humility—wifely virtues that should guarantee success within the institution of patriarchal marriage—does not escape us, particularly since Shakespeare visually and orally places such emphasis on them. Her response to Othello's physical blow, "I will not stay to offend you," is amplified, sympathetically, by Lodovico—"Truly, an obedient lady"—then, sneeringly, by Othello: "she's obedient, as you say, obedient; / Very obedient" (4.1.247–56). Barbary's self-effacement in the willow song lyric—" 'Let nobody blame him, his scorn I approve' " (4.3.52)—is but an echo of Desdemona's: " 'Tis meet I should be us'd so, very meet" (4.2.107); "My love doth so approve him, / That even his stubbornness, his cheeks, his frowns— / . . . have grace and favor in them" (4.3.19–21). The infinite capacity for giving of herself evident in her obedience and humility is at last concentrated in the generosity of forgiveness. She forgives both the unknown villain who wrongs her—"If any such there be, heaven pardon him!" (4.2.135)—and the husband who murders her: "Nobody; I myself. . . . / Commend me to my kind lord" (5.2.124–25). The depth and totality of her emotional commitment is such that, having deliberately chosen Othello for her husband, she bears the consequences of that choice in a way that reanimates the meaning of the words, "for better, for worse," from the traditional wedding ceremony. Her devotion is as unchanging as her purity and innocence are absolute.

Desdemona's absolute innocence of the act of adultery is all that is necessary to make the point of Othello's mistake—her absolute purity and devotion are not. Shakespeare, I believe, exploits the absoluteness of her purity to accentuate the degree of Othello's mistake. Likewise, he exploits the absoluteness of her devotion to accentuate the contrast between Othello's reaction to his imagined mistreatment by her and her reaction to her real mistreatment by him. Shakespeare thus portrays a love that, like the charity of Cordelia, surpasses understanding in its ability and willingness to subsume individual needs to the demands of a bond with another. If in tragedy as in romantic comedy self-knowledge is achieved through learning how to love, then the self-knowledge of Desdemona—like that of Juliet and the female protagonists of the romantic comedies before her and Cordelia after her—is a donné of the drama. Whether or not the male protagonist is capable of achieving self-knowledge through learning how to love is the question that reverberates throughout the unfolding dramatic action.

The nature of Desdemona's love for Othello depends in part upon her response to his cruel treatment of her. Either she is self-deceiving or she is as honest with herself as she is with her father and her husband. If she continues to love Othello because she denies his cruelty, her love is not an idealized love. If she continues to love him despite her admission and acceptance of that cruelty, her love is an idealized love, indeed. But there is no greater degree of ambivalence surrounding the nature of her love, I believe, than there is surrounding her characterization. That is not to bring us full circle back to those critics who would simplify her character into an abstraction of Good, vying with an Evil Iago for the soul of Othello in a Jacobean version of a medieval morality play—one that happens to be focused in the bedroom. But it is to take issue with those critics who find fault in her dissembling over the stolen handkerchief: "It is not lost" (3.4.83). To condemn Desdemona for this fearful lie, or for her determination in bringing Cassio's suit, or for her incidental mention of Lodovico in the willow song scene, or indeed, for marrying Othello in the first place,[12] requires, it would seem, a mentality not unlike that of Iago. To find Desdemona "guilty" of these small "crimes" or to seek in them any complicity in or responsibility for the larger crime of her murder not only reveals an appetite for red herrings; it is perverse, and demonstrates the lengths to which critics are prepared to go to avoid the ineluctable truth of the plot—Othello murders an innocent Desdemona.

The problem is, rather, that the dramatic action exhibits Desdemona's inalterable love in the central situation—Othello's loss of faith—in which she is acted upon rather than acting. It is true that after her choice of husband, her interaction with her father, and her argument for accompanying Othello to Cyprus—in the essentially comic action of the first two acts of the play—she does not appear to originate a series of events by a deliberate choice. The comic action of the first half of the play emphasizes her independence and courage; the tragic action of the last half of the play stresses her purity and innocence. The divided Desdemona of which I speak—a split between character and construct—is significant because it goes to the heart of the larger question concerning Shakespeare's female protagonists.[13] Integrity is inflected in the comedies in the autonomy and wit of a Portia, a Beatrice, a Rosalind, a Viola, an Olivia. These traits are mitigated but not eliminated in the tragedies, where integrity is inflected instead in the moral excellence of a Cordelia or a Desdemona. In both *Lear* and *Othello,* as Doran points out, "the characters in whom we feel the greatest moral strength are not the heroes, although they are both good men, but the heroines—the daughter Cordelia and the wife Desdemona." If the female protagonists are silenced and victimized by the tragic action, it is to raise questions about the destructive forces that bring about that silencing and victimizing. Cordelia and Desdemona are both destroyed, Doran concludes, because "the failure to understand their evident goodness by the father and husband who should know them best engulfs them in the deadly scheming malice of ambitious and evil men" (1976, 146).

Although act 3 forces the audience to view Desdemona from Othello's perspective, Shakespeare alters impressions of character when he shifts perspectives in act 4. We no longer look at her and her imagined mistreatment of Othello through his eyes; we look at men and their real mistreatment of women through her eyes, and those of Bianca and Emilia. Our apprehension of Desdemona's characterization as the embodiment of moral excellence deepens into understanding as the tragic action develops, controlling our responses to that action. The locus of moral strength in her character both magnifies the masculine impulses of insecurity—Othello's—and misogyny—Iago's—that dominate act 3 and theatrically represents the subjectivity of women that Bianca and Emilia mirror in acts 4 and 5. Shakespeare exploits the fiction of Desdemona's betrayal of Othello to accentuate the reality of his betrayal of her. Our final impression is not the innocent Othello victimized by the cruel Iago, but the innocent Desdemona victimized by the cruel Othello.

Shakespeare's invention of the character of Bianca is one of the more significant transmutations of his source material. In Cinthio's *Gli hecatommithi*, Cassio is a married man who emerges "one dark night from the house of a courtesan with whom he used to amuse himself" when he is attacked by Iago ([1566] 1973, 249). From this hint Shakespeare omits Cassio's wife and creates Bianca. Obviously her dramatic function is not to provide local color or to give us a flavor of night life on this military outpost on Cyprus. Her presence expands the theme of men's treatment of women, particularly that which is dramatized in the central relationship—of a husband who believes his wife to be a whore. Both Bianca and Emilia serve as dramatic contrasts to Desdemona, as critics generally recognize, but in their treatment by the men in their lives and in their attitudes toward those men, they serve as parallels as well.[14]

Baldly put, Bianca is Bianca because Iago is Iago. Women in *Othello* are, as the arc of the tragic action emphasizes, what men make them. Initially she seems to be merely a reflection of Othello's mistaken notion of Desdemona—paramour, courtesan, whore. She may be seen as supplying "in living form on the stage," to quote Mack, "the prostitute figure that Desdemona has become in Othello's mind" ([1960] 1970, 340).[15] Her role is transitional in nature: Cassio's mistreatment of Bianca contrasts with Othello's early treatment of Desdemona and parallels his later mistreatment of her. She enters the action immediately following the deception scene, dramatizing the state of mind of a soldier who—either accustomed to a lifetime of military victory and defeat or by nature disposed to action and impatient with deliberation—perceives reality in terms of absolute polarities. Whatever the reason, a consciousness such as Othello's has little room for doubt, as the deception scene makes clear. Desdemona falls straight from the status of chaste wife to that of whore. And at the point when, in Othello's mental imagery, Desdemona becomes "the soliciting whore," Mack maintains, Bianca enters "in the flesh" ([1960] 1970, 340).

We might agree that Bianca is no more than a manifestation of Othello's false image of Desdemona were she not completely lacking in sensuality. While Othello's jealousy is focused exclusively on the sexual, Shakespeare has no interest in characterizing women solely by this aspect of human behavior. What is striking, rather, is the disparity between Cassio's view of Bianca and her self-evaluation, the gap between the shallowness of his feeling for her and her genuine affection for him. She reiterates Desdemona's response to Othello in her willingness to "be circumstanc'd" and in her good-natured humor. Cassio's lie, "Not that I love you not," prompts her quick retort: "But that you do not love me" (3.4.196). Her obedience to his wish that she copy the handkerchief parallels Desdemona's and Emilia's obedience to their husbands. Conversely, her change of mind emphasizes the constancy of Desdemona's obedience: "What did you mean by that same handkerchief you gave me even now? I was a fine fool to take it. I must take out the work? . . . I'll take out no work on 't" (4.1.148–55). Bianca is consistent, though, in placing a value on her affections and her identity that is different from her worth in men's eyes: "I am no strumpet, but of life as honest / As you that thus abuse me" (5.1.122–23).

Cassio is not Iago's superior in his ability to distinguish women into two categories—chaste virgins such as Desdemona and "courtesans" such as Bianca—because his distinction depends on Iago's filthy premise. It is impossible to trust "either the adoring or the degrading perspective," as Cook puts it (1980, 191). Cassio's conversation with Iago reveals a man who does not take seriously the woman he beds: he refers to her as "customer," "monkey," "bauble," and "fitchew," echoing in a minor key the obscene epithets Othello hurls at Desdemona. He alternately ridicules Bianca (in her absence) and is embarrassed by her affections (in her presence). The disparity between Cassio's mistreatment of Bianca and her sincere feelings for him broadens the critique on male treatment of females that is centered in the relationship of the protagonists. The contrast between his courtly idealization of Desdemona and his casual denigration of Bianca—particularly in view of the theatrical representation of these women on stage—makes clear the inadequacy of his splintered vision. His split perspective focuses on two separate women; Othello's focuses on Desdemona alone. Cassio "divides women into two types, Desdemona and Bianca," observes Greene, "but Othello directs his confusions at one woman, his wife" (1979, 21). Such reductive, splintered visions as these are simpler alternatives for both men than any recognition of the complex subjectivity presented by the women in their lives.

Shakespeare further alters *Gli hecatommithi* when he fills in the outlines of Emilia's character sketched by Cinthio: "this false man had likewise taken to Cyprus his wife, a fair and honest young woman. Being an Italian she was much loved by the Moor's wife, and spent the greater part of the day with her" ([1566] 1973, 243). Although initially her dramatic function, like that of Bianca, would seem to be one of contrast, her characterization grows in significance until her defiance of Iago in the final scene defies his view of women throughout the play.

When we enter the willow song scene, we enter a world of women from which men are excluded. For a brief moment the door of the bedchamber shuts out masculine fantasizing about women—the "phantasmagoric questioning, raving, mocking debate" of which Stilling speaks (1976, 159). Women are represented as neither objects of male desires nor fragments of male delusions. Desdemona's virtues of honesty, kindness, and loyalty are repeated in a lower key, as Doran notes, in Emilia (1976, 146). As the two women indulge in quiet, intimate conversation with one another, the reasons for Emilia's fierce attachment to Desdemona throughout the play become clear. The emphasis two scenes before her murder on "the alabaster innocence of Desdemona's world," to quote Mack ([1960] 1970, 334)—on her total lack of preparation for what is happening to her—renders it one of the most poignant scenes in the tragedies. Desdemona's own articulation of the very view that is responsible for her condemnation and murder heightens its poignancy: "Dost thou in conscience think . . . / That there be women do *abuse* their husbands / In such gross kind?" (4.3.61–63, italics mine). The worldly humor of Emilia's response emphasizes her characteristic practicality and shrewdness but does not conceal the generosity of motive that so often characterizes Shakespeare's female figures: "for all the whole world—'ud's pity, who would not make her husband a cuckold to make him a monarch? I should venture purgatory for 't" (4.3.75–77). The willow song scene is one of those scenes of spiritual cross purposes, Mack maintains, which appear toward the close of a Shakespearean tragedy. In the two opposed voices of Desdemona and Emilia "the line of tragic speech and feeling generated by commitment" is crossed by "an alien speech and feeling very much detached" ([1960] 1970, 334). Like the gritty accents of the Clown echoing between the lines of Cleopatra's exultation, those of Emilia sound between the lines of Desdemona's innocence.

Emilia's forthright discussion of human sexuality views it as neither male "appetite" for females—Iago's credo—nor wives' "abuse" of husbands—Othello's delusion. It emphasizes instead the shared traits of both sexes of the human animal:

> Let husbands know
> Their wives have sense like them; they see, and smell,
> And have their palates both for sweet and sour,
> As husbands have. What is it that they do
> When they change us for others? Is it sport?

> I think it is. And doth affection breed it?
> I think it doth. Is 't frailty that thus errs?
> It is so too. And have not we affections,
> Desires for sport, and frailty, as men have?

$$(4.3.93-101)$$

Emilia's emphasis on the similarity of female and male needs creates an impression of balance, reciprocity, and equality within relationships between the sexes. The partnership model for heterosexual relations that emerges from this speech is suggested by the denotations of the Latin roots of the word *conjugal,* in sharp contrast to the dominator model that is suggested by the Latin roots of the words *marriage* and *marry.*[16] She voices an attitude of moderation that is painfully absent in the play—a middle ground between the extremes of Desdemona's purity and innocence, on the one hand, and Othello's insecurity and Iago's misogyny, on the other. Emilia's articulation of the female point of view echoes another minority view, that of Shylock:

> Hath not a Jew eyes? Hath not a Jew hands, organs, dimensions, senses, affections, passions; fed with the same food, hurt with the same weapons, subject to the same diseases, heal'd by the same means, warm'd and cool'd by the same winter and summer, as a Christian is? If you prick us, do we not bleed? If you tickle us, do we not laugh? If you poison us, do we not die?
>
> (*The Merchant of Venice*, 3.1.59–66)

Shylock's self-justification contributes to the exposé of Christian treatment of Jews that is implicit throughout the comic action of *The Merchant of Venice.* Similarly, Emilia's defense of the female sex finally makes explicit the critique of male treatment of females that is implicit throughout the tragic action of *Othello.*

The power of Emilia's argument, like that of Beatrice in *Much Ado,* is allowed utterance, but because Shakespeare's emphasis is on destroyed innocence in this play, its only audience is the female protagonist in the confinement of her bedchamber. It has no impact on the tragic action bearing down on Desdemona from the male realm. Although Emilia voices the precise corrective to Iago's misogyny, the attitude that has the potential to prevent catastrophe, it has no chance of reaching and affecting the deluded male protagonist until it is too late. This is tragedy, not comedy. Unlike Dogberry and the bumbling Watch, who manage against all odds to convey the truth to the point it eventually impinges on the potentially tragic action of *Much Ado,*

Emilia simultaneously learns of Iago's villainy and reveals it to Othello. But Desdemona is dead.

Reconciling Emilia's practicality and shrewdness with her status as Iago's wife presents a problem—one that is mitigated, however, by her utter ignorance of his villainy until the final scene. The disparity between his hatred of her and her desire to please him, like the gap between the feelings of Cassio and Bianca for one another, further broadens the critique on male treatment of females in the play. Her obedience to his wish that she steal the handkerchief, "I nothing but to please his fantasy" (3.3.299), parallels Bianca's obedience to Cassio's wish that she copy it. The obedience of both women doubly mirrors Desdemona's compliant devotion to Othello. Emilia's defiance of Iago, conversely, like Bianca's of Cassio, accentuates the unchanging obedience, humility, generosity, and forgiveness of Desdemona. Shakespeare's emphasis on Emilia's defiance of her husband necessarily dispels any doubt that lingers about her ignorant complicity in his plot:

> *Iago.*   Go to, charm your tongue.
> *Emilia.* I will not charm my tongue; I am bound to speak.
>   My mistress here lies murthered in her bed— . . .
>   And your reports have set the murder on. . . .
> *Iago.* What, are you mad? I charge you get you home.
> *Emilia.* Good gentlemen, let me have leave to speak.
>   'Tis proper I obey him; but not now.
>   Perchance, Iago, I will ne'er go home. . . .
> *Iago.* 'Zounds, hold your peace.
> *Emilia.*   'Twill out, 'twill out! I peace?
>   No, I will speak as liberal as the north:
>   Let heaven and men and devils, let them all,
>   All, all, cry shame against me, yet I'll speak.
> *Iago.* Be wise, and get you home.
> *Emilia.*   I will not.
>
>   (5.2.183–223)

Four times Iago attempts to exercise the prerogatives of patriarchal marriage and commands his wife to silence or to her house. Four times, as though exhilarated by the power of language, Emilia defies him with the truth before she pays the price for that defiance with her life. Like her beloved mistress, she dies by her husband's hand.

Emilia's instruction of Othello prompts merely a discovery of his mistake about Desdemona's innocence of adultery rather than any psychological self-knowledge. He reveals the attenuated nature of his

moment of truth: he would be "an honorable murderer . . . / For
naught I did in hate, but all in honor" (5.2.294–95). The judicial
review of the case by all the characters on stage finally leads, as
Heilman puts it, to "the hero's self-recognition in error (discovery of
his 'mistake' if not complete discovery of himself)" (1956, 161).
Ornstein is less parenthetical in distinguishing between discovery of
error and gain of insight: "it is not clear that Othello gains a new or
greater wisdom from murdering Desdemona. Though he recovers
enough of his former stature to admit that he is an 'honourable
murderer,' he learns only the simple truth which was obvious to the
coarse Emilia, to Cassio, and even at last to the foolish Roderigo—
that Desdemona was chaste" ([1960] 1965, 228). The reappearance of
Paris—the parody of Romeo's early self—at the Capulet vault emphasizes Romeo's ennoblement. The reappearance of Lodovico—the representative of civilized Venice—accentuates the degeneration of
Othello's nobility:

> Is this the noble Moor whom our full Senate
> Call all in all sufficient? Is this the nature
> Whom passion could not shake? whose solid virtue
> The shot of accident nor dart of chance
> Could neither graze nor pierce?
>
>   (4.1.264–68)

In *Othello*, as in *Hamlet*, revenge is consummated, with the difference that Hamlet takes vengeance upon Claudius while Othello
takes vengeance upon himself. His final act is not shocking because
we feel—despite the influence of Iago—that Othello is guilty. In
response to Desdemona's affirmation and reaffirmation of faith that
are expressions at once of self-confidence and courage, the best
Othello is capable of offering in return is self-assertion in the form of
self-destruction.

Shakespeare's comic treatment of the story of the true woman
falsely accused in *Much Ado* exposes the inadequacy of male constructions of females; his tragic treatment of the same story in *Othello*
plumbs greater psychological depths to emphasize the degradation of
those who would presume to possess another human being. To search
either *Romeo and Juliet* or *Othello* for evidence that endorses or
condemns the male protagonist's nobility or ignobility is to miss the
larger commentary on sexual possession. Male concern with possession is inflected in both the Petrarchan and the Ovidian discursive
traditions that Shakespeare inherits, as well as in the institution of
patriarchal marriage that characterizes his culture. Male concern with

possession underlies the Petrarchan stance away from which Juliet draws Romeo. It animates the prerogatives of patriarchal marriage and erupts in Iago's misogyny, both of which debase Othello despite the healing influence of Desdemona. Neither Romeo's participation in the Petrarchan discursive tradition nor Othello's participation in the institution of patriarchal marriage, and, under Iago's influence, the Ovidian discursive tradition, allows for the possibility of a mutual relationship between the two whole selves. These discourses and institutions are inadequate because they reduce and objectify the female: romantic desire requires a male lover to glorify the physical appearance of a female beloved; patriarchal marriage requires a husband's honor to depend upon a wife's chastity. These gaping inadequacies suggest the viability of another option—a partnership between equals such as that which Emilia articulates—that is freed of the constraints of all three.

4

Antony and Cleopatra: Female Subjectivity and Orientalism

> She's beautiful and she's laughing.
> —Hélène Cíxous, "The Laugh of the Medusa"

Whereas military action is relegated to the background in *Othello*, it is interwoven into the love story in *Antony and Cleopatra*. The intricate alternation of scenes of war and scenes of love, in fact, makes the obtrusion of the feud upon the love story in *Romeo and Juliet* (3.1) appear somewhat mechanical by contrast. Indeed, the loose structure of the play, especially the quick, frequent shift of scene throughout acts 3 and 4, has drawn criticism. Nor does *Antony and Cleopatra* share the atmosphere of domesticity of *Othello*. The larger political context is not confined to the Venetian Senate and reports of battles off stage—it determines the action. Like Marlowe's *Dido, Queen of Carthage,* as Roger Stilling points out, Shakespeare's play represents "a clash between the values of empire and the values of love" (1976, 278). Whereas Aeneas chooses empire, however, Antony chooses love.

The impulses of possession and power—held to the level of petty social rivalry in *Romeo and Juliet,* turned inward and concentrated in Iago's nihilism in *Othello*—are set loose in *Antony and Cleopatra* to rule the entire known western world. There is no Iago-like exploitation, manipulation, or teasing out of masculine attitudes as in *Othello*. Instead, they are embedded in the very foundation of empire and are freely expressed by every male character in the play. Because of their preoccupation with imperial ideals, Roman men—Philo, Antony, Enobarbus, Octavius, Agrippa, Pompey, Menas, Canidius, Scarus— disparage love, sex, and women, although Antony and Enobarbus stand apart from the others in their capacity to idealize as well.

Beginning with Philo's opening slurs on the protagonists, much of the play offers an exposition of the dominant ideology of male Roman superiority and female Egyptian inferiority:

Nay, but this dotage of our general's
O'erflows the measure. Those his goodly eyes,
That o'er the files and musters of the war
Have glow'd like plated Mars, now bend, now turn
The office and devotion of their view
Upon a tawny front; his captain's heart,
Which in the scuffles of great fights hath burst
The buckles on his breast, reneges all temper,
And is become the bellows and the fan
To cool a gypsy's lust. Look, where they come!
Take but good note, and you shall see in him
The triple pillar of the world transform'd
Into a strumpet's fool. Behold and see.

                                                        (1.1.1–13)

Yet here we have something new, not just a patriarchal construction of
gender difference as in *Othello* and *Romeo and Juliet,* but an imperialistic construction of cultural difference. Cleopatra, therefore—before we have met her—undergoes a series of double reductions. Her
status is diminished not merely to that of a whore, or "strumpet," but
to that of an alien, or "gypsy." Her body is reduced by synecdoche
not merely to her woman's part, or "front," but to that of a particular
racial hue, "tawny." As imperialists, Romans are, of course, required
to revile Cleopatra as the colonized other.[1] And, good representative
of the empire that he is, Philo perfectly articulates the ideology of his
dominant culture. He is no more capable of seeing the relationship
between Cleopatra and Antony as the love of a woman and a man for
one another than he is capable of mythologizing Cleopatra as a
Venus, although he is capable of valorizing Antony as a "plated
Mars." Because Philo views the world in strictly political and military
terms, he sees his "general," his "captain," his "triple pillar of the
world" reduced to the status of a "fool" by the "lust" of a "gypsy."
Cleopatra, as the mysterious cultural other, is endowed with a sexuality so powerful it has the effect of emasculating Antony. As Queen
of Egypt, she represents what Freud calls "the dark continent" of
female sexuality—Africa—and, as such, is the source of profound
anxiety to the Romans.

Because the Roman ideology angrily expressed by Philo in the
opening lines of the play is insisted on throughout the dramatic
action, it is not difficult to understand why so much critical response
to *Antony and Cleopatra* strikes so moralistic a note. Schücking,
Stoll, and their followers represent an approach to the play that is
more responsive to the political plot and the outer military experience

it conveys—ideals of honor and duty, empire and war—than it is to the play's poetry.[2] In this view, the protagonists are seen largely through Philo's eyes: the whore Cleopatra is responsible for Antony's fall from indisputably honorable Roman ideals.

This view is problematic, however, because it more accurately describes the moralism of Shakespeare's source, Plutarch's *The Life of Marcus Antonius*, than his dramatization of that source. And, as we know, whenever Shakespeare draws on a single source for his story—in *Antony and Cleopatra* as in *Othello* and *Romeo and Juliet*—he transforms conventional morality. Time and again he takes what strikes the author of his source "as being the whole moral bearing of the story," as Kermode puts it, and delimits its place in his play, placing it in conflict with other issues or subordinating it to them (1974, 1056). Michael Goldman, for one, takes issue with the critical view that "th' expense of spirit in a waste of shame" is the emblem of the lovers' relationship. This sentiment describes "*not* what happens between Antony and Cleopatra," he insists, but rather "the typical *Roman* view of sex in the play" (1985, 121–22, my italics). In allowing the skeptics in the play the full expression of their views, Shakespeare quite disarms criticism, as Janet Adelman points out. The entire drama is, in effect, "a test of the lovers' visions of themselves," she observes; "if the imaginative affirmations were not so persistently questioned, they could not emerge triumphant" (1973, 110).

Immediately following the sentiments of Philo, Shakespeare allows the sentiments of the lovers:

> *Cleopatra.* If it be love indeed, tell me how much.
> *Antony.* There's beggary in the love that can be reckon'd.
> *Cleopatra.* I'll set a bourn how far to be belov'd.
> *Antony.* Then must thou needs find out new heaven, new earth.
> (1.1.14–17)

A. C. Bradley, G. Wilson Knight, and their followers represent an approach that is more responsive to the play's poetry and the inner psychological experience it conveys—imagination and creativity, pleasure and love—than to the military plot.[3] Critics such as Mack, therefore, emphasize phases of the male protagonist's psychic change—delineation, conflict, and recovery—rather than the phases of external action—exposition, conflict, crisis, catastrophe, and so on ([1960] 1970, 342 and 335). In this view Cleopatra, rather than being seen in Roman terms as a whore, is often glorified as an archetype of the eternal feminine principle. She offers Antony an alternative vision of life that rivals, even surpasses, that of Rome. Rarely is she humanized, though, or seen as a woman whose love ennobles Antony in the way Juliet's love ennobles Romeo and Desdemona's love has the potential to ennoble Othello, or seen as a subject in her own right.

Androcentrism

Shakespeare consistently associates the idea of nobility not with military deeds but with personal bonds, from Antony's declaration in the opening scene that "the nobleness of life / Is to do thus" (1.1.36–37) as he embraces Cleopatra, to her vision of Antony at her death: "I see him rouse himself / To praise my noble act" (5.2.284–85). While Cleopatra's final statement is consistent with the depth and totality of her emotional commitment to him throughout the play, however, Antony's emotions are at first ambivalent. While he speaks extravagantly of Cleopatra and himself as "a mutual pair" (1.1.37), mutuality between the two lovers is in fact impossible. Until he extricates himself from the complex web of Roman ideology—interwoven with its beliefs in male Roman superiority and female Egyptian inferiority—any equality between partners, upon which mutuality depends, is impossible.

Antony, a middle-aged libertine who has enjoyed years of revelry with Cleopatra and, no doubt, other women before her, is no novice in love. But like Romeo, he, at first, is unable to make an authentic emotional commitment; like Othello, he attempts to apply the values of military experience to the realm of intimate relationships. He participates in both idealizing Petrarchan discourse, as does Romeo, and denigrating Ovidian discourse, as does Othello. Desire for Cleopatra and revulsion for her conflict with one another, therefore, making Antony's response to her more ambivalent than that of either Romeo to Juliet or Othello to Desdemona. Roman constructions of gender difference—Petrarchism and Ovidianism—are complicated by Roman constructions of cultural difference—or, what Edward Said calls *Orientalism*. *Orientalism* is to culture as Petrarchism and Ovidianism are to gender. All three are constructions of colonized or sexual others by imperialistic or patriarchal dominant ideologies.[4] All three Roman constructions of other operate powerfully, from Philo's opening lines, throughout the play.

A grandiose tone marks Antony's earliest declaration on the worlds of Rome and Egypt that tug at his conscience and vie for his allegiance: "Let Rome in Tiber melt, and the wide arch / Of the rang'd empire fall! Here is my space" (1.1.33–34). His sentiments seem utterly honest, true to himself and true to Cleopatra. Yet we feel that

Antony does not understand the love of which he speaks with such hyperbole. It is obvious at the beginning of the play that he does not know Cleopatra, as Robert Ornstein notes, that he "does not yet know what is evident to the audience, that his only desire is to be with this woman" ([1966] 1967, 398).[5] The action of the love story charts his discovery of the "new heaven, new earth" of which he speaks so uncomprehendingly in his first utterance in the play. His (re)orientation from an autonomous to a relational perspective allows him in the end to apprehend a humanized Cleopatra.

Antony's romantic hyperboles barely conceal his deeper need for escape from Roman duty in epicurean enjoyment of sensual pleasures:

> Now for the love of Love, and her soft hours,
> Let's not confound the time with conference harsh;
> There's not a minute of our lives should stretch
> Without some pleasure now. What sport tonight?

> (1.1.44–47)

He holds a Roman view of sex early in the play; his appetite for Cleopatra, therefore, is not unlike his appetite for food, drink, and revelry. The emphasis on Antony's appetitive nature continues these traits from *Julius Caesar*, of course.[6] Yet it suggests as well a level of development—that of self-interest—from which he evolves.[7] The emphasis on his enjoyment of sensual pleasures suggests not only his utter incompatibility with the "holy, cold, and still" Octavia but his potential for a fuller emotional life as well. His capacity for giving is as great as his capacity for consuming, and it is this generosity that the power of Cleopatra's imaginative command immortalizes after his death. In the early Antony are revealed attitudes and responses to love that are not simplified, but complicated with maturity; they do not constrict but dilate with age.

The most evocative description of Cleopatra in the play, of course, is that of Enobarbus, not Antony. His set piece on the lovers' meeting at Cydnus reveals and elicits—rather than Philo's political and sexual revulsion—fascination. It is an invitation to rise above the delimiting Roman constructions of cultural and gendered other—what Phyllis Racklin calls "these inferior modes of perception"—and, instead, to participate in "the imaginative vision of the poet" (1972, 204).[8] His description of Cleopatra on her barge is appreciative of her uniqueness:

> The barge she sat in, like a burnish'd throne,
> Burnt on the water. The poop was beaten gold,

Purple the sails, and so perfumed that
The winds were love-sick with them; the oars were silver,
Which to the tune of flutes kept stroke, and made
The water which they beat to follow faster,
As amorous of their strokes. For her own person,
It beggar'd all description: she did lie
In her pavilion—cloth of gold, of tissue—
O'er-picturing that Venus where we see
The fancy outwork nature.

(2.2.191–201)

He most closely approaches the truth when he describes Cleopatra in paradoxical terms: "Age cannot wither her, nor custom stale / Her infinite variety" (2.2.234–35). Yet even this poetic tribute gives way to a more ordinary Roman view of her sexuality. Her complexity— her totality of being—is imagined merely as her capacity to defy masculine appetite: "Other women cloy / The appetites they feed, but she makes hungry / Where most she satisfies" (2.2.235–37). His extravagant homage to Cleopatra contains distant echoes of the courtly love tradition, indeed, echoes of Romeo's compliments to Rosaline's beauty and sexual frustration at her chastity.

That Enobarbus does not have a higher view of Cleopatra or of women than do other Romans is evident in his earliest advice to Antony: "Under a compelling occasion, let women die. It were pity to cast them away for nothing, though between them and a great cause, they should be esteem'd nothing" (1.2.137–40). No matter how significantly Cleopatra figures in Antony's life while he indulges in the pleasures of Egypt, her value is minuscule compared to imperial issues. Antony's vows of devotion in her presence yield in her absence to expressions of guilt about his dereliction of Roman duty:

These strong Egyptian fetters I must break,
Or lose myself in dotage. . . .
                    The present pleasure,
By revolution low'ring, does become
The opposite of itself. . . .
I must from this enchanting queen break off;
Ten thousand harms, more than the ills I know,
My idleness of doth hatch. . . .
She is cunning past man's thought. . . .
Would I had never seen her!

(1.2.116–52)

He appeals to the idea of duty to justify leaving her, using a Roman language and tone similar to that of Philo.

Roman constructions of woman are several, but all are objectifications of male desire. Women are objects that satisfy men's sexual
appetites; they are prizes of war; they are political pawns to be used as
the means of cementing opportunistic alliances. Conflicting with the
political rejection and wish to eliminate Cleopatra—the view most
forcefully articulated by Philo—is a fascination with and even desire
for her. Although despised by the Romans, Cleopatra obviously
operates powerfully upon their imaginations. Politically she may be
peripheral to the business in Rome, but symbolically she is central:

> *Enobarbus.*   . . . you had then left unseen a wonderful piece of work,
>   which not to have been blest withal would have discredited your travel.
>   (1.2.153–55)

> *Caesar.*   Let's grant it is not
>   Amiss to tumble on the bed of Ptolomy. . . .
>
>   (1.4.16–17)

> *Agrippa.*   Royal wench!
>   She made great Caesar lay his sword to bed;
>   He ploughed her, and she cropp'd.
>
>   (2.2.226–28)

> *Antony.* I' th' East my pleasure lies.
>
>   (2.3.41)

> *Pompey.*   . . . your fine Egyptian cookery
>   Shall have the fame. I have heard that Julius Caesar
>   Grew fat with feasting there.
>
>   (2.6.63–65)

> *Enobarbus.* He will to his Egyptian dish again.
>
>   (2.6.126)

As these passages reveal, the Roman opinion of her is unanimous.
Viewed from an androcentric perspective, Cleopatra is but the supreme erotic delight among the vast array of exotic experiences that
the conquest of diverse cultures offers up to the policemen of the
empire. Viewed from a gynocentric perspective, however, it is obvious that she exists for Rome as a projection of its own sexuality—as,
to quote Peter Stallybrass and Allon White in another context, the
"primary eroticized constituent of its own fantasy life" (1986, 5).[9]
Politically reviled *and* sexually desired, then, Cleopatra is the source
of profound ambivalence for all the Romans, although Antony dimly

apprehends a Cleopatra that is object of neither repugnance nor fascination.

Like his fellow Romans, Octavius, too, wishes to possess Cleopatra, but his desire is not for a sexual possession. Military defeat reduces all—cultures and cities, peoples and individual human beings—to spoils of war.[10] What Octavius pants for is to keep Cleopatra alive as a war trophy, even as she is determined to deny him this aim in their final battle of wills and wits. He has no doubt of her corruptibility because he believes it to be a characterizing trait of her sex: "Women are not / In their best fortunes strong, but want will perjure / The n'er-touch'd vestal" (3.12.29–31).[11] Despite his flattery about her honor and his lies about her future, however, his behavior is governed by the imagined spectacle of Cleopatra as the chief prize of his victory over Antony and the guarantor of his Roman immortality. Seduced by the spectacle of his own glory rather than by her, he is capable only of envisioning that "her life in Rome / Would be eternal in our triumph" (5.1.65–66). The threats of Proculeius and the warnings of Dolabella reveal this intention to Cleopatra:

Proculeius.   Cleopatra,
Do not abuse my master's bounty by
Th' undoing of yourself. Let the world see
His nobleness well acted, which your death
Will never let come forth.

                                (5.2.42–46)

Dolabella.   Though he be honorable,—
Cleopatra. He'll lead me then in triumph?
Dolabella. Madam, he will, I know 't.

                                (5.2.108–10)

Dolabella.   Caesar through Syria
Intends his journey, and within three days
You and your children will he send before.

                                (5.2.200–2)

Octavius's use of flattery, lies, and threats to dissuade Cleopatra from killing herself obviously conflicts with the references to his "nobleness" and "honor." The Roman discourse of honor, here, as elsewhere in the play, clashes with the dishonorable acts that it would mask.

The women of Rome are as subject to degradation as are women of the colonies as the handling of Octavia's marriage to Antony discloses. In Plutarch, she is an active, persuasive figure whose diplomacy affects the behavior of Octavius and Antony (1964, 278, 282–83, 288–93). In Shakespeare, however, she is a sacrificial victim upon the altar of political ambition; her conciliatory words have no power over either Roman. Why does Shakespeare make this alteration in his source? It is a puzzling one for a writer who characteristically ameliorates or enhances the female characters in his source material. It is plausible that here, as in the history plays, Shakespeare uses women "who seem the most at the mercy of the male world," as Dusinberre puts it, "to assert values which measure its worth and find it wanting" (1975, 293).

Agrippa's words make clear that the marriage is but an opportunistic device:

> To hold you in perpetual amity,
> To make you brothers, and to knit your hearts
> With an unslipping knot, take Antony
> Octavia to his wife. . . .
>   By this marriage,
> All little jealousies, which now seem great,
> And all great fears, which now import their dangers,
> Would then be nothing.
>
> (2.2.124–33)

The marriage he proposes is, in effect, "not between Antony and Octavia," as Stilling points out, "but between Antony and Octavius" (1976, 282).[12] Perhaps Antony is led on by Octavius's lieutenants because he seeks to pay homage in his return to Rome to the ideals of nobility and honor of a bygone republic. He is as capable as his fellow triumvir, however, of traducing the ideal of honor by using it to justify dishonorable action.

Octavius, in the calculating manner that marks his every move, is capable of cynically marrying his sister to his enemy and then using the occasion of her abandonment as an excuse to wage war against that enemy.[13] His first words to Antony use the fact of Antony's marriage to Fulvia to "patch a quarrel": "Your wife and brother / Made wars upon me, and their contestation / Was theme for you; you were the word of war" (2.2.42–44). It comes as no surprise, then, that Octavius exploits the occasion of Octavia's abandonment to make his move against Antony: "You are abus'd / Beyond the mark of thought; and the high gods, / To do you justice, makes his ministers / Of us and those that love you" (3.6.86–89). Antony, for his part, is capable of speaking of his honor as he packs Octavia off to Rome, "If I lose mine honor / I lose myself" (3.4.22–23), even as he is later capable of berating Cleopatra for having seduced him from a marriage that he never honored:

> Have I my pillow left unpress'd in Rome,
> Forborne the getting of a lawful race,
> And by a gem of women, to be abus'd
> By one that looks on feeders?
>
> (3.13.106–9)

As these passages make clear, it is not Antony's liaison with the Queen of Egypt but his marriage to the sister of Caesar that causes the rift between the two triumvirs. It is not his relationship to Cleopatra but his political marriage—"his flirtation with Caesar's rather than with Cleopatra's values," as Marsh maintains—that brings about his political overthrow (1976, 167).

Throughout the tragedy Octavius is the epitome of the politician, "always a bad word in Shakespeare," as Kermode wryly notes (1974, 1345). The most accurate description of the atmosphere of political instability and treachery that prevails in his empire, significantly, is his own: "he which is was wish'd, until he were; / And the ebb'd man, ne'er lov'd till ne'er worth love, / Comes dear'd by being lack'd" (1.4.42–44). Shakespeare's plays often emphasize the instability of male ideals, such as those of Octavius's empire, by juxtaposing them to the stability of female values. Viewed from an androcentric perspective, women in the plays are "the grievous survivors of wars men make and die in," as Dusinberre puts it. Viewed from a gynocentric perspective, however, women stand for "permanence and fidelity against shifting political sands" (1975, 294).[14] When the primary motivation of marriage is political, in Rome as in the history plays, it is degrading. When its vows of commitment between two individuals are used to cement political alliances, it does not promote stability. Against the crudeness of the Roman view of women and the humiliating tratment of Octavia as a pawn in a chess game between two men, Shakespeare represents the possibility of a intimate relationship that is honorable, heroic, and noble.

Gynocentrism

In the comedies, Shakespeare focuses on the female view of heterosexual relations; in the tragedies, he focuses on the male view. In *Antony and Cleopatra*, however, even more so than in *Othello* and *Romeo and Juliet*, he forcuses equally on the female view. Lear's nausea at his daughters' sexuality and Hamlet's contempt for his mother's frailty are absent even though Antony's repeated alienations from Cleopatra recall the sexual possessiveness and jealousy of Othello. One reason the love relationship in *Antony and Cleopatra* is more complex than that in either *Othello* or *Romeo and Juliet* is that Cleopatra is even more fully realized as a sexually active woman than are either Desdemona or Juliet. Yet that is not to say that it is the representation of Cleopatra as an object of Roman sexual fantasies that is relevant. It is, rather, Shakespeare's representation of her sexual subjectivity that is significant.

Shakespeare's comic and tragic explorations of ideals of love intermingle in *Antony and Cleopatra*. Although the first half of the play forebodes tragedy, as Bradley notes, it is not decisively tragic in tone. "Certainly the Cleopatra scenes are not so," he says. We read them and we witness them "in delighted wonder and even with amusement" ([1909] 1964, 222–23). This comic atmosphere prevails in the Egyptian scenes in acts 1 and 2 that portray Cleopatra trying to convince Antony to stay; Cleopatra left with her women and longing for him; Cleopatra receiving news of his marriage; Cleopatra questioning the messenger about Octavia. To give up the battle with time and live intensely in the present is, Barbara Everett remarks, "to create a small and circumscribed area in which to exist, in an exhilarated moment of freedom and vitality" (1964, xxxvi). It is a way or vision of life that is more native to comedy, of course, than to tragedy. It is the way of *jouissance,* or pleasure, that Cleopatra lives and breathes in every fiber of her being.[15]

Rosalind's stinging advice to Phebe, "Sell when you can, you are not for all markets" (*As You Like It,* 3.5.60), urges females, because aging devalues the "product," not to be too coy lest they alienate their potential "customers." But Cleopatra has no regard (no more than Desdemona or Juliet) for Rosalind's strategy. Where Juliet should play hard to get, she is instead forthright in declaring her love: "I'll prove more true / Than those that have more coying to be strange" (*Romeo and Juliet,* 2.2.100–1). Conversely, Cleopatra knows that to hold Antony's interest she must intrigue him and keep him off balance. Those critics who dislike her build their case for her scheming, deceptive nature by fastening on her exchange with Charmian. To the advice, "In each thing give him way, cross him in nothing," Cleopatra responds, "Thou teachest like a fool: the way to lose him" (1.3.9–10). Indeed, it is possible to see her at the outset of the drama as implementing this principle, as attempting to get Antony to stay in Egypt by encouraging him to leave for Rome. Five times she urges Antony to listen to the messages from Rome. To his, "Grates me, the sum," she answers, "Nay, hear them, Antony" (1.1.18–19); to his, "Let's not confound the time with conference harsh," she responds, "Hear the ambassadors" (1.1.45–48). The effect of her words, however, is to undercut his escapist attitude. Cleopatra is down-to-earth. Her accessions of realism, as Rosalie Colie points out, "puncture Antony's simplistic view of love and Cleopatra as satisfaction to his appetite" (1974, 188).

Always underlying Cleopatra's humor is an awareness of the disparity between broad declarations of love and authentic emotional commitment. Her rejoinder, "Excellent falsehood! / Why did he marry Fulvia, and not love her?" (1.1.40–41), pierces Antony's inflated talk of "a mutual pair." She is mindful as well of his view of marriage and pleasure as antipodal experiences. Married to Fulvia, he enjoys his "pleasure" in Egypt; declaring "here is my space" to Cleopatra, he deserts her for Rome; married to Octavia, he leaves her for Egypt. Beneath Cleopatra's mocking tone is cognizance that Antony's unfeeling response to Fulvia's death is an indication of his possible treatment of her:

> O most false love!
> Where be the sacred vials thou shouldst fill
> With sorrowful water? Now I see, I see,
> In Fulvia's death, how mine receiv'd shall be.
>
> (1.3.62–65)

Despite his romantic hyperboles she is fully aware of the political expediency of his actions: "Good now, play one scene / Of excellent dissembling, and let it look / Like perfect honor" (1.3.78–80). Her ironical common sense "pierces her own theatricals," as Colie notes; she knows herself, she knows Antony, and she knows the precarious, politicking world she lives in (1974, 189).

Shakespeare emphasizes the ease of Antony's betrayal of Cleopatra by enclosing it between scenes that accentuate her loyalty to him: her response to Antony's absence (1.5), to the news of his remarriage (2.5), and to reports of his new wife (3.3). Perhaps it is the alternating lyrical and farcical humor of these scenes that causes critics to overlook the fact of her devotion to him. The void of his absence adumbrates the void of his death. Both drain life of meaning. Her reluctance to remain conscious after his departure for Rome—"Give me to drink mandragora. . . . / That I might sleep out this great gap of time / My Antony is away" (1.5.4–6)—anticipates her reluctance to remain alive after his death: "Shall I abide / In this dull world, which in thy absence is / No more than a sty?" (4.15.60–62). Her imaginings of his every move fill the void: "Where think'st thou he is now? Stands he, or sits he? / Or does he walk? Or is he on his horse? / O happy horse, to bear the weight of Antony!" (1.5.19–21). She speaks knowingly, of course, as someone who has borne the weight of Antony. We do not miss the irony of her imagining her name on Antony's lips—"He's speaking now, / Or murmuring, 'Where's my serpent of old Nile?'" (1.5.24–25)—because he never speaks her name in Rome. Nor do we miss the irony of her reference to herself as a trader in love—"Give me some music; music, moody food / Of us that trade in love" (2.5.1–2)—because it follows the political business of Octavius cynically trading Octavia to Antony.

Aside from the more obvious humor and ironies of the Alexandrian scenes in the first three acts, their lightness and comedy also derives from Cleopatra's complete lack of possessiveness. Despite the full expression of her insecurity in response to Antony's departure for Rome and the news of his remarriage, what is striking in her actions and speech is the absence of any sense of possession or ownership on her part or any complaint of failed obligation on his part. Similarly, while critics inevitably note Antony's magnanimity, generosity, and forgiveness, particularly that toward his soldiers in the last half of the play, they overlook Cleopatra's refusal to berate him for his repeated acts of disloyalty and mistrust.

Although the protagonists in Shakespeare's romantic comedies and love tragedies are flesh and blood, the stuff that attracts and binds men and women to one another in a relationship surpasses sexual desire. While sex obviously is an integral element of her relationship with Antony, Cleopatra is nothing like the cunning sensualist that the Romans (and some critics) imagine. Shakespeare does not represent a lusting Cleopatra. Rather, he represents a woman who has a range of interests and a man who, if we agree with Irene Dash, thinks only of lovemaking (1981, 214). Cleopatra's dialogues with Antony are devoted to talk of politics and battle, to alienations and reconciliations. Despite Pompey's lewd jokes, Maecenas's lusty appetite for stories of her, and Agrippa's lip-smacking interruptions of Enobarbus's poetic tribute to her, Shakespeare does not depict her as an object of Roman sexual fantasies. While the text of *Antony and Cleopatra* is laden with sensual and sexual innuendos, any genuinely erotic moments in the play are not Roman fantasies about Cleopatra, but Cleopatra's *jouissance*: her pleasurable recollection of her revelries with Antony, for example, during his absence in Rome and her orgasmic revery of joining him in death. As opposed to the delimiting Roman construction of Cleopatra, moreover, her longing for Antony is "not of the flesh," as Ornstein emphasizes, "but of the total being" ([1966] 1967, 391). If the Roman view insists on reducing her to a "strumpet" and "gypsy," her awareness of Antony's humanity enlarges him: he is "the demi-Atlas of this earth, the arm / And burgonet of men" (1.5.23–24). She is conscious of his potential for something more than a once noble Roman of a once honorable republic living out the sentence of Octavius's corrupt empire.[16] Cleopatra alone is aware of this potential on his part. Included in her awareness of Antony's "well-divided disposition," his alternating "sadness" and "merriness," his oscillating alienation from her and connection to her is an awareness of his profoundly Roman ambivalence toward Egypt and toward her. Yet also included in her awareness of Antony's "heavenly mingle" is an awareness of his capacity for surpassing Roman ideals: "He was not sad, / . . . he was not merry, / . . . but between both. / O heavenly mingle!" (1.5.53–59).

Rigid constructions of masculinity and femininity are as crucial to empire as are constructions of dominant and colonial cultures; the two, as we have seen, are intricately bound up in one another in this play. Any blurring of the boundary between the sexes gives the Romans considerable anxiety because it undermines or even threatens to expose the myths of male Roman superiority and female Egyptian inferiority for what they are. The disparaging tone of Octavius at his initial entrance and his first mention of the lovers is unmistakable. The news from his spies in Alexandria reveals to him that Antony "fishes, drinks, and wastes / The lamps of night in revel" (1.4.4–5). It is the fact that Antony and Cleopatra indulge in the pleasures of the orient together, though, that is most disturbing to Octavius. Curiously, the shared nature of the lovers' activities has the effect, for Octavius, of emasculating Antony, while at the same time, disconcertingly for Octavius, masculinizing Cleopatra. Antony "is not more manlike / Than Cleopatra, nor the queen of Ptolomy / More womanly than he" (1.4.5–7). All of male Rome exhibits a similar regard for rigidly gendered experience. The rumors that Enobarbus relates to Cleopatra object to the intervention in war by those who clearly do not belong there: " 'tis said in Rome / That Photinus an eunuch and your maids / Manage this war" (3.7.13–15). Later Enobarbus sees Antony's ability to move his troops to tears as neither the manipulative oratory of a practiced politician nor the genuine feeling of a man increasingly aware of the relational aspect of his nature. Instead, he sees it as the ability to induce female weakness: "Look, they weep, / And I, an ass, am onion-ey'd. For shame, / Transform us not to women" (4.2.34–36).

The lovers' references to a blurring of the boundary between the sexes, on the other hand, are playful in tone and reveal flexible notions of maleness and femaleness. Their exchange of clothes is cause for Cleopatra's delighted recollection: "I drunk him to his bed;

/ Then put my tires and mantles on him, whilst / I wore his sword Philippan" (2.5.21–23).[17] Antony remarks in a similar vein as he embraces her after military victory: "leap thou, attire and all, / Through proof of harness to my heart, and there / Ride on the pants triumphing!" (4.8.14–16).[18] The point is made even in the trivial detail of Cleopatra's preference in billiards partners. She would play Mardian as soon as Charmian: "As well a woman with an eunuch play'd / As with a woman" (2.5.5–6). More significant is her motive for fighting at Actium. Whereas in Plutarch her motive is suspicion of Antony's betrayal (1964, 291–92), in Shakespeare it is political responsibility: "A charge we bear i' th' war, / And as the president of my kingdom will / Appear there for a man" (3.7.16–18). Her insistence on fighting by Antony's side echoes Desdemona's insistence on accompanying her husband to Cyprus. Antony reiterates Othello's reference to Desdemona as his "fair warrior" when he refers to Cleopatra as his armorer: "Thou fumblest, Eros, and my queen's a squire / More tight at this than thou" (4.4.14–15). At rare moments of felicity such as these, both soldiers describe their relationship with their lovers in military terms.

Cleopatra's desire to participate in the male realm of battle is profoundly disturbing to the Romans. Enobarbus may joke that Fulvia's warlike spirit makes sex a desirable diversion from battle: "Would we had all such wives, that the men might go to wars with the women!" (2.2.65–66). But he would not have Cleopatra fight at Actium. He voices anxiety at the thought of female intervention, and more particularly, at the power of female sexuality to disrupt battle: "If we should serve with horse and mares together, / The horse were merely lost; the mares would bear / A soldier and his horse" (3.7.7–9). Echoing Philo in perpetuating the myth of the sexualized, colonized other, Enobarbus not only reduces Cleopatra to the sexual and the bestial. He further endows her with the power to reduce the Romans to the sexual and the bestial in a scenario in which she transforms the classic, organized field of battle into a grotesque, chaotic field of copulating bodies.[19] Canidius and Scarus see Antony's flight from battle less metaphorically, as an emasculating experience: "our leader's led, / And we are women's men" (3.7.70–71); "Experience, manhood, honor, ne'er before / Did violate so itself" (3.10.22–23). Yet Shakespeare contests the adequacy of Roman ideals of masculinity, as of femininity.

Oscillation

When Shakespeare devotes acts 3 and 4 of *Antony and Cleopatra* to three military battles between the two triumvirs and three quarrels between the two lovers, he forces upon the audience the question of the relationship between the diverse realms of human experience— love and war. It is nearly impossible to discern whether Antony's oscillation between insecurity and confidence in love causes his alternating military fortunes, or whether his alternating military defeat and victory cause his oscillation in love.

Time and again Antony expresses his conflict with Octavius as that between age and youth. He refers to this disparity in positive terms when he feels confident and in negative terms when he feels insecure. In moments of confidence Antony sees his conflict with Octavius as one between a man and a boy, between mature and immature masculinity, and between military experience and inexperience. The repeated references of both lovers to Octavius's immaturity, in fact, reveal their contempt for the emotional, relational sterility he represents:[20]

> *Cleopatra.*   . . . who knows
>   If the scarce-bearded Caesar have not sent
>   His pow'rful mandate to you. . . .
>
> (1.1.20–22)

> *Antony.* To the boy Caesar send this grizzled head,
>   And he will fill thy wishes to the brim
>   With principalities. . . .
>   . . .tell him he wears the rose
>   Of youth upon him; from which the world should note
>   Something particular. His coin, ships, legions,
>   May be a coward's, whose ministers would prevail
>   Under the service of a child as soon
>   As i' th' command of Caesar.
>
> (3.13.17–25)

In moments of insecurity, however, Antony seems to fear the virility of a younger Octavius and to fear his own impotence as an older man. He insists on fighting Octavius by sea despite his soldiers' warnings that his ships are not well manned. When Canidius asks "Why will my lord do so?" he responds, significantly, "For that he [Octavius] dares us to 't" (3.7.29). Octavius's dare catches at Antony's vulnerable ego like a barb; caught, he must disprove the sense of inadequacy that is disclosed in his repeated references to immature and mature masculinity. Octavius, incapable of any similar feelings of insecurity or inadequacy, is caught by neither Antony's challenge to single combat nor his challenge to wage battle at Pharsalia (3.7.30–32). Antony's chivalric challenge—"I dare him . . . / To lay his gay comparisons apart, / And answer me declin'd, sword against sword, / Ourselves

alone" (3.13.25–28)—and Octavius's response—"these offers, /
Which serve not for his vantage, he shakes off" (3.7.32–33)—signify
the conflict between Roman values old and new, between honor and
opportunism, between desperation and cold practicality.

The pattern of Octavius's and Antony's mutual challenges and
responses reflects the issues of the political plot—the reduction of two
triumvirs to one. One of them fixes his eyes on the end and uses
everything and everyone as a means to that end; the other has no such
singleness of aim (Bradley [1909] 1964, 225). Antony's sense of vulnerability lies in his shifting values, in his disorientation from Roman
ideals, and his (re)orientation to Egyptian ideals. It also lies in his
disentanglement from Roman constructions of Cleopatra and Egypt
as sexual and cultural other and his discovery of a human connection
with the woman, Cleopatra, beneath the myth that is Cleopatra. As
his autonomous self erodes, there is nothing to replace it until he
discovers his relational self.

The lovers' alienations from one another, or more accurately, Antony's repeated lapses of belief in Cleopatra, are characterized by self-
loathing on his part combined with anger directed at her. But every
alienation is followed by reconciliation. Disgust and anger repeatedly
melt into forgiveness in a pattern, we feel, most closely approximating
day-to-day relations between any two lovers. Unlike the linear pattern of *Othello* (or *Troilus and Cressida*), this cyclical pattern of
repetition of *Antony and Cleopatra* grants the lovers the ability, as
Marianne Novy puts it, to "recreate their relationship after its apparent destruction" (1984, 122). The repetition of the estrangements
between the protagonists has the further effect of suggesting the
gradual change in Antony. The position he comes to as a result of each
of these episodes—after Actium, after the Thidias episode, after the
final defeat—is always one we recognize as "more noble than the one
he has taken in disgust," as Goldman notes, "more appealing, more in
keeping with that great property which should be Antony's" (1985,
122).

Antony's first lapse of belief in Cleopatra after Actium focuses as
sharply on the disparity between past and present, between remem-
bered victory and fresh defeat, as it does on her. The memory of the
battle at Philippi, where his experience dominated Octavius's inexperience, pricks at his ego, tormenting him:

>   . . . he at Philippi kept
> His sword e'en like a dancer, while I strook
> The lean and wrinkled Cassius, and 'twas I
> That the mad Brutus ended. He alone

Dealt on lieutenantry, and no practice had
In the brave squares of war. . . .

(3.11.35–40)

Imaginative recollection operates powerfully throughout the play; the heroic values of a bygone Rome are lost except through Antony's vivid memory of them. Here as elsewhere recollection of past heroism only accentuates his present humiliation: "Now I must / To the young man send humble treaties, dodge / And palter in the shifts of lowness" (3.11.61–63).

Although Rome is now corrupt, Antony has difficulty disentangling himself from its values. The dishonor of defeat is so shattering that it brings not only his reputation but his whole identity into question: "I / Have lost my way for ever. . . . / I have fled myself. . . . / I have lost command" (3.11.3–23).[21] As he earlier uses the temptation of Cleopatra to excuse his dereliction of Roman duty, he now finds emotional relief by placing blame upon her. He says to his men, "I follow'd that I blush to look upon" (3.11.12); he says to her:

O, whither hast thou led me, Egypt? See
How I convey my shame out of thine eyes
By looking back what I have left behind
'Stroy'd in dishonor. . . .

(3.11.51–54)

His insistence on Cleopatra's awareness of his emotional dependency on her—an act of projection—serves, of course, to emphasize his own dawning awareness of the same:

> Egypt, thou knew'st too well
My heart was to thy rudder tied by th' strings,
And thou shouldst tow me after. O'er my spirit
Thy full supremacy thou knew'st, and that
Thy beck might from the bidding of the gods
Command me. . . .
> You did know
How much you were my conqueror, and that
My sword, made weak by my affection, would
Obey it on all cause.

(3.11.56–68)

His incipient understanding of her significance in his life is an indication of the change in him. The lovers are reconciled when her forthright acknowledgment of fear—"Forgive my fearful sails! . . . /

O my pardon! . . . / Pardon, pardon!" (3.11.55–68)—is matched by
his generous response: "Fall not a tear, I say, one of them rates / All
that is won and lost" (3.11.69–70).

The Thidias episode dramatizes Antony's second alienation from
Cleopatra. It also emphasizes her continued loyalty to him and
Enobarbus's betrayal of him. That she remains loyal is not surprising;
it is inconceivable, given her complete devotion to him in every word
and deed, that she behave in any other way. The rich sarcasm of her
response to Octavius's messenger is unmistakable:

> *Thidias.* He [Octavius] knows that you embrace not Antony
>   As you did love, but as you fear'd him.
> *Cleopatra.*   O!
> *Thidias.* The scars upon your honor, therefore, he
>   Does pity, as constrained blemishes,
>   Not as deserved.
> *Cleopatra.*   He is a god and knows
>   What is most right. Mine honor was not yielded,
>   But conquer'd merely.
>
>   (3.13.56–62)

Cleopatra is as acutely aware here as she is after Antony's death that
Octavius's avowal of concern for her honor is a lie.[22]

What the episode does reveal is the inadequacy of Roman constructions of Egypt and Cleopatra. Enobarbus's suspicion of her
political betrayal and Antony's suspicion of her sexual betrayal both
contribute to the exposure. Shamed by military defeat into thoughts
of desertion, Enobarbus readily misinterprets the exchange between
Thidias and Cleopatra. He says to himself that he will desert Antony
because she does: "Sir, sir, thou art so leaky / That we must leave thee
to thy sinking, for / Thy dearest quit thee" (3.13.63–65). The fact of
the lovers' second reconciliation does nothing to alter his course.
Antony, for his part, again expresses his sense of disorientation as a
threatened loss of identity: "I am / Antony yet" (3.13.92–93). He is
again painfully aware of the disparity between past reputation and
present humiliation: "he [Octavius] seems / Proud and disdainful,
harping on what I am, / Not what he knew I was" (3.13.141–43). Yet
his obsession fastens less on the fiction of her political conniving than
on the fiction of her sexual betrayal. It is Thidias's kiss of her hand
that prompts his rage of sexual jealousy: "To flatter Caesar, would
you mingle eyes / With one that ties his points?" (3.13.156–57). He
turns on her as Othello turns on Desdemona:

> Ah, you kite! . . .
> You have been a boggler ever. . . .

I found you as a morsel, cold upon
Dead Caesar's trencher; nay, you were a fragment
Of Cneius Pompey's. . . .

                                            (3.13.89–118)

Both men are keenly aware of the humiliation of being cuckolded. Othello seeks relief in the thought that cuckoldry is inescapable: "this forked plague is fated to us / When we do quicken" (*Othello*, 3.3.276–77). Antony raises his humiliation to mythological proportions: "O that I were / Upon the hill of Basan, to outroar / The horned herd!" (3.13.126–28).

Cleopatra's simple question—"Not know me yet?" (3.13.157)—deflates Antony's emotional turmoil. He cannot, however, understand her without understanding himself. After he vents his wrath on her, as Goldman points out, "she wins him back to her and to himself" (1985, 122). Antony is untrue to himself when untrue to Cleopatra, true to himself when true to her. His awakening and response to her love embodies the paradoxical truth that love offers the possibility of both the greatest absorption in the lover and the deepest awareness of the self. Cleopatra expresses an awareness of their interdependency directly and simply: "It is my birthday. / I had thought t' have held it poor; but, since my lord / Is Antony again, I will be Cleopatra" (3.13.184–86). Her remark on the change in him echoes Mercutio's remark on the change in Romeo: "now art thou Romeo; now art thou what thou art" (*Romeo and Juliet*, 2.4.89–90). Even as Cleopatra celebrates her birthday, Antony, like Romeo after meeting Juliet, is in the process of undergoing a transformation, of shifting from one phase of identity to another. And his recognition of her love has the immediate effect of buoying him up; renewed confidence in love contributes to renewed confidence of war—he is victorious in the next day's battle.

The defeat at Actium and the Thidias episode suggest that military defeat profoundly undermines Antony's confidence in love. Conversely, his only military victory is suffused in his confidence in love. He reveals this confidence in his departure from Cleopatra before battle: "O love, / That thou couldst see my wars to-day, and knew'st / The royal occupation, thou shouldst see / A workman in 't" (4.4.15–18). And he reiterates it in his joyous greeting of her afterward: "O thou day o' th' world, / Chain mine arm'd neck, leap thou, attire and all, / Through proof of harness to my heart, and there / Ride on the pants triumphing!" (4.8.13–16). His elated words are more intimate in tone than grandiose; his embrace, in contrast to that at the opening of the play, is an honest expression of his love, not an extravagant gesture.[23] Cleopatra beings him back from a moment in which "he

feels his greatness is gone," Goldman maintains, to one in which
"we—and his audiences on stage—feel that he is exercising it again"
(1985, 122).

Just before Antony's "triple turn" or third lapse of belief in
Cleopatra, Scarus describes his wildly oscillating swings of emotion:
"Antony / Is valiant, and dejected, and by starts / His fretted fortunes
give him hope and fear / Of what he has, and has not" (4.12.6–9).
Antony does not lead his navy, but overlooks the battle from a
hillside; his interpretation of events turns, significantly, on a non
sequitur. His description of his navy's betrayal sounds like an accurate
enough depiction of the scene before him: "My fleet hath yielded to
the foe, and yonder / They cast their caps up and carouse together /
Like friends long lost" (4.12.11–13). His projection of blame for their
betrayal onto Cleopatra, however, marks a departure from experien-
tial reality: "This foul Egyptian hath betrayed me" (4.12.10). The
illogicality of the passage reveals more about his state of mind, of
course, than the scene before him. He blames her for the defeat at
Actium because she flees battle in fear; he blames her for the final
defeat even though there is no indication that she is present in battle.
The only indication in the text, in fact, is that she is *not* present:
"Swallows have built / In Cleopatra's sails their nests" (4.12.3–4).
Antony, therefore, occupies a position midway between Othello,
who requires "ocular proof" to sustain the fiction of Desdemona's
betrayal, and Leontes, who needs none at all to sustain the fiction of
Hermione's betrayal.

Antony's insistence upon viewing Cleopatra in these terms is a
twisted distortion of the heartfelt desire to fight at his side that she
voices earlier. Yet his third and final outburst of rage at her is not
wholly surprising in a man whose shifting confidence and insecurity
in love and war mirror and magnify one another. Military vulnerability collapses into sexual vulnerability; he imagines himself at
the moment of military defeat as victim of the combined treachery of
both lover and enemy:

> Triple-turn'd whore! 'tis thou
> Hast sold me to this novice. . . .
> The witch shall die.
> To the young Roman boy she hath sold me. . . .

(4.12.13–48)

Antony's jealousy focuses not on Octavius's factotum as in the Thidias
episode, but on Octavius himself. References to his enemy's youth
again erupt in this context: "this novice," "blossoming Caesar," "the

young Roman boy." Once more he imagines Cleopatra's political betrayal in sexual terms, finding Othello's emotional relief in calling his lover "whore." In the posture of impotent victim of their conspiracy, he pictures his connection to her not in human terms—his emotional dependency on her, as earlier—but instead, in mythological terms—her power over him. He, therefore, resorts to the Roman construction of the myth of Cleopatra, taking up Philo's imperialistic discourse of fear and revulsion for the cultural other. She is not like Desdemona merely "whore," but rather, a threat, a mystery, a supernatural entity: "this grave charm," "thou spell," "most monster-like," a "witch."

Cleopatra's one utterance in the scene—"Why is my lord so enrag'd against his love?" (4.12.31)—pierces through Antony's irrational invective. Like her earlier question—"Not know me yet?"—it echoes Desdemona's bewildered response to the accusations of her husband. If Antony's repeated rages are insufficient to expose the tenuousness of his belief in her, then her bewilderment at his behavior makes the point. So out of character is he—so unlike his true self—that she thinks (and we think) that "he's more mad / Than Telamon for his shield, the boar of Thessaly / Was never so emboss'd" (4.13.1–3). Shakespeare presents male delusions about female betrayal in *Antony and Cleopatra* as in *Othello* only to accentuate the reality of female constancy and to expose male inconstancy.[24]

Intersubjectivity

If any sense of greatness exists in *Antony and Cleopatra*, it is primarily as the command over the imaginations of other characters, as Goldman maintains; "it depends on what people think of you and what you think of yourself" (1985, 113). The long concluding movement of the play is dominated by a series of what he calls "imaginative transformations" which bring about a "corresponding emotional movement of enhancement—from meanness and agitation of spirit to generosity and peace."[25] These range from Antony's final outburst of rage and Cleopatra's response, through the false report of her death and his attempted suicide, to his death in her arms and the final spectacle of her death (1985, 128).

The lie of Cleopatra's death is not one of her own making. Contrary to her earlier repudation of Charmian's advice, she now follows it. After the length and the intensity of Antony's final rage, her willingness, even innocence, in resorting to such a solution does not strike us as strange. In its impact upon the dramatic action—prompting the male protagonist's death by suicide—the device of her false death reiterates that of Juliet. In its regenerative effect upon the repentant male protagonist, it reiterates and anticipates the deaths and resurrections of such female protagonists as Hero, Helena, Thaisa, Imogen, and Hermione in the comedies and the romances. Antony approximates Othello in his wish for the death of his lover: "one death / Might have prevented many. . . . / The witch shall die. . . . / She dies for 't" (4.12.41–49). Because Shakespeare's interest in *Antony and Cleopatra*, as in *King Lear* and *The Winter's Tale*, is in the regeneration of the male protagonist, however, the emphasis is on the reconciliation between the lovers. Antony represents in this play, therefore, a line of male protagonists that extends from the romantic comedies through the love tragedies to the romances.

The change in Antony is apparent in his poetic meditation upon the clouds just moments before he receives the news of Cleopatra's death. It is one of the play's great "emblems of transformation" (Goldman 1985, 126). No longer acting out any soldierly role, he speaks more to himself than to Eros. His final expression of his sense of loss of military identity, therefore, reveals no regard for audience:

> Sometime we see a cloud that's dragonish,
> A vapor sometime like a bear or lion,
> A tower'd citadel, a pendant rock,
> A forked mountain, or blue promontory
> With trees upon 't that nod unto the world,
> And mock our eyes with air. Thou hast seen these signs,
> They are black vesper's pageants. . . .
> That which is now a horse, even with a thought
> The rack dislimns, and makes it indistinct
> As water is in water. . . .
>
> (4.14.2–11)

His reflection upon the clouds draws an equation between himself and their ephemeral nature: "My good knave Eros, now thy captain is / Even such a body. Here I am Antony, / Yet cannot hold this visible shape" (4.14.12–14). Paradoxically, though, as Goldman points out, even while Antony claims that he has lost command, the passage reveals the power of his imaginative command. The feeling of the passage contradicts its logic, so that not a sense of weightlessness but instead a sense of solidity dominates our impressions. "We are not meant to feel an insubstantial Antony here, but a weighty one" (1985, 126–27).

There is something in the quality of Cleopatra's references to

Antony that is lacking in the quality of his references to her until he thinks she is dead. His response to the false report of her death reveals a man who, in coming to terms with her death, finally comes to terms with his life:

> Unarm, Eros, the long day's task is done,
> And we must sleep. . . .
> I will o'ertake thee, Cleopatra, and
> Weep for my pardon. So it must be, for now
> All length is torture; since the torch is out.
> Lie down and stray no farther. Now all labor
> Mars what it does; yea, very force entangles
> Itself with strength. Seal then, and all is done.
>
> (4.14.35–49)

The simplicity of statement and intimacy of tone with which he expresses his singular desire to join his lover—"I will o'ertake thee, Cleopatra"—echoes that of Romeo: "Juliet, I will lie with thee tonight" (*Romeo and Juliet*, 5.1.34). But Antony has cause, as Romeo does not, to weep for pardon. While Lear and Leontes undergo prolonged suffering or years of remorse, Antony's change of heart is immediate.

The paradox that Antony becomes "a fuller man in his decline," as Ornstein puts it ([1966] 1967, 397), is understandable when we consider the dual pattern of the dramatic action. Even as he loses all in the conquest of empire, he gains immeasurably in his quest into the realm of emotional intimacy. As he loses his autonomous self, he finds his relational self. He is a "mine of bounty" to his men; his familiarity and ease with his soldierly identity allow him the confidence necessary for the expression of his generosity in this arena. His magnanimity is revealed in the detail of his treatment of Eros—"I did make thee free" (4.14.81)—as well as in his self-incriminating response to the desertion of Enobarbus:

> . . . send his treasure after; do it,
> Detain no jot, I charge thee. Write to him
> (I will subscribe) gentle adieus and greeting;
> Say that I wish he never find more cause
> To change a master. O, my fortunes have
> Corrupted honest men!
>
> (4.5.12–17)

The coffers of his largesse are often empty when it comes to Cleopatra, however, as his repeated rages emphasize. His unfamiliarity and unease with his emerging identity of lover deny him the confidence necessary for the expression of his generosity. In the end, however, he treats Cleopatra as he treats Enobarbus; he is no less generous and forgiving of the woman he loves than he is of the man he loves. He treats her as neither detestable "whore" nor supernatural "witch" but as an equal, and it is this change in Antony that allows for the possibility of a mutual, reciprocal exchange between two partners in love that was impossible earlier. Antony and Cleopatra become at last "the mutual pair" of which he speaks so extravagantly—and uncomprehendingly—at the beginning of the play. Both lovers make explicit the nature of their relationship at their deaths, proclaiming their bonds to one another in marital terms: Antony declares, "I will be / A bridegroom in my death" (4.14.99–100), as he attempts to run himself through; Cleopatra declares, "Husband, I come!" (5.2.287), as she applies the asps to her breast.

The multiple references to the nobility and honor of love interpenetrating the play culminate in the final tributes to one another of Enobarbus, Antony, and Cleopatra. In the end, Enobarbus embodies the value of honor in love, not war. His potential for change is suggested throughout the drama. He epitomizes Roman cynicism about women, yet Cleopatra's "infinite variety" elicits from him the most poetic tribute to her in the play. He epitomizes Roman control of emotions, yet he dies out of love for Antony rather than fight "in the van" against him:

> O Antony,
> Nobler than my revolt is infamous,
> Forgive me in thine own particular,
> But let the world rank me in register
> A master-leaver and a fugitive.
>
> (4.9.18–22)

His cynicism, so useful while he holds his career and everyone and everything around him in the comic focus of detachment, as Mack points out, "withers in the face of his engagement to ultimate issues" ([1960] 1970, 328). Enobarbus dies heartbroken, speaking with the same density of feeling as the lovers.

Antony says, "Since Cleopatra died / I have liv'd in such dishonor that the gods / Detest my baseness" (4.14.55–57), yet he is not a man who has lost all as he prepares to take his life. Deeply moved by Cleopatra's and Eros's deaths, he is inspired by their nobility. He knows Cleopatra well; he intimates her attitude toward Octavius and her own death precisely, as the final moments of the play bear out:

> I, that with my sword
> Quarter'd the world, and o'er green Neptune's back
> With ships made cities, condemn myself to lack
> The courage of a woman—less noble mind
> Than she which by her death our Caesar tells,
> "I am conqueror of myself."
>
> (4.14.57–62)

Eros appears in the tragedy just before Antony's suicide so that he may kill himself rather than kill Antony, eliciting this response:

> Thrice-nobler than myself!
> Thou teaches me, O valiant Eros, what
> I should, and thou couldst not. My queen and Eros
> Have by their brave instruction got upon me
> A nobleness in record. . . .
>
> (4.14.95–99)

His name and his deed echo in a minor key the other deaths for love (Mack [1960] 1970, 328).

The final reconciliation of the alienated lovers is one of those resonant scenes, like the reunion of Desdemona and Othello at Cyprus, that allows us to partake of several dimensions of emotional and artistic experience at once. The reunion at the monument reminds us of the male protagonist below and the female protagonist above in the orchard scene in *Romeo and Juliet*. Both of these scenes, in turn, reiterate the image of the woman at the window that permeates the courtly romance tradition. Indeed, the physical elevation of Antony on stage to the level of Cleopatra emblematizes his ennoblement. He sees himself at his death as "the greatest prince o' th' world, / The noblest" (4.15.54–55), and she echoes his description. His generosity is at last concentrated in a lack of possessiveness and a concern for her welfare. His dying words are devoted to her making peace with his enemy: "Of Caesar seek your honor, with your safety" (4.15.46). The selflessness of his devotion to Cleopatra, together with his solicitude for her welfare, echoes the altruism of the speaker in Sonnet 71: "No longer mourn for me when I am dead / . . . for I love you so, / That I in your sweet thoughts would be forgot / If thinking on me then should make you woe."[26] Antony experiences compassion; his participation in the suffering of another—Cleopatra as well as Enobarbus and Eros—is the mark of his humanity.

The reunion at the monument enables Antony to die in Cleopatra's arms. In Lear's entry with Cordelia's body critics see an inversion of the pietà; the emblem of Cleopatra embracing the dying Antony conflates the grief of the pietà and the nurturance of the Madonna. Yet Christian emblems such as these are but appropriations of older cultures, such as images of Isis, Osiris, and Horus in Egyptian iconography (Campbell 179). Cleopatra's extraordinary use of humor discloses the intimacy of the lovers: "Noblest of men, woo 't die? / Hast thou no care of me?" (4.15.59–60). She feigns selfishness, echoing Juliet's response to Romeo's death: "O churl, drunk all, and left no friendly drop / To help me after?" (*Romeo and Juliet*, 5.3.163–64). Cleopatra lives beyond Antony's death in one last enactment of loneliness, desolation, and mourning: "Shall I abide / In this dull world, which in thy absence is / No better than a sty?" (4.15.60–62). Her description of the utter void left by his death has the solidity and weight of Antony's sense of loss at his moment of greatest desolation in 4.14:

> O, see, my women:
> The crown o' th' earth doth melt. My lord!
> O, wither'd is the garland of the war,
> The soldier's pole is fall'n! Young boys and girls
> Are level now with men; the odds is gone,
> And there is nothing left remarkable
> Beneath the visiting moon.
>
> (4.15.62–68)

Like Antony, she is describing loss. Even while she says that life is drained of meaning, however, the audience is again subject to the power of imaginative command. The feeling of the passage, as earlier, defies its logic. There is no greater representation of female theatrical subjectivity in Shakespeare's plays than Cleopatra, and nowhere is that subjectivity represented more powerfully than in Cleopatra's response to Antony's death.[27]

To the soldier Antony is the pole star by which a course can be charted, "an image that suggests both the brightness of his glory and the seeming impossibility of his fall," as Marsh maintains (1976, 191–92). But the image also suggests the dependency on him of those around him. In love as in war, for Cleopatra as for his men, Antony is the pole star. His emotional dependency on her is matched and balanced by her dependency on him in a continuous, reciprocal, attracting and counterattracting, responsive and counter-responsive interrelationship. This is not to ignore the sexual innuendo of the "soldier's pole." But Cleopatra's image reminds us of the absoluteness of the "ever-fixed mark" of Sonnet 116 "that looks on tempests and is never shaken; / It is the star to every wand'ring bark, / Whose worth's unknown, although his highth be taken." The artist possesses the ability to "make [love] a permancy," E. M. Forster maintains, despite the reality that "all history, all our experience, teaches us that no human relationship is constant." An intimate relationship is as unstable as "the living beings who compose it, and they must balance like jugglers if it is to remain" ([1927] 1985, 55). In Antony's oscillation and Cleopatra's depth and totality of emotional commitment, Shakespeare represents both the human capacity for instability and the capacity for constancy in intimate relations.[28]

Shakespeare's outrageous artistic choice—killing off the male protagonist in act 4 and devoting act 5 to the female protagonist—has drawn critical attention and provoked negative response, especially from those incapable of understanding or accepting the "unique compliment," as Bradley puts it, he pays Cleopatra ([1909] 1964, 235–236).[29] In Shakespeare's greatest departure from Plutarch, he devotes act 5 to her poetic celebration of Antony and her determination to die. Her death is at once an act of defiance of Octavius and an enactment of marital union to Antony. Her dealings with Octavius dramatize the turn of her back on this world; her poetic tribute to Antony anticipates her eager embrace of him in the next. Remarkably, yet quite like all her earlier scenes, her last scenes are characterized by "an expression of ineffaceable lightheartedness," as Everett puts it— one that evokes a mood closer to the experience of the comedies than the tragedies (1964, xxiv). Cleopatra is given, as Cameo Moore claims, "the theatrical license to destabilize the tragic genre" (1989).

Even as Cleopatra's humor punctures Antony's easy romanticizing earlier in the play, the power of her imaginative command immortalizes him. She achieves the effect that the persona in Sonnet 55 so deliberately intends: "Not marble nor the gilded monuments / Of princes shall outlive this pow'rful rhyme." Her earlier references to Antony as "the demi-Atlas of this earth, the arm / And burgonet of men," "the crown o' th' earth," and a "huge spirit" culminate in her portrait of him as a colossus:

His face was as the heav'ns, and therein stuck
A sun and moon, which kept their course, and lighted
The little O, th' earth. . . .
His legs bestrid the ocean; his rear'd arm
Crested the world; his voice was propertied
As all the tuned spheres, and that to friends;
But when he meant to quail and shake the orb,
He was as rattling thunder.

(5.2.79–86)

His capacity for giving is such that each act of magnanimity and forgiveness of both Cleopatra and Enobarbus makes him not a diminished but a greater figure:

> For his bounty,
> There was no winter in 't; an autumn it was
> That grew the more by reaping. His delights
> Were dolphin-like, they show'd his back above
> The element they liv'd in. In his livery
> Walk'd crowns and crownets; realms and islands were
> As plates dropp'd from his pocket.
>
>   (5.2.86–92)

The paradox of his infinitely renewing generosity echoes that of the infinite bounty that Juliet so eloquently proclaims (*Romeo and Juliet*, 2.2.133–35). Cleopatra envisions the infinitude of Antony's "bounty" in seasonal and cosmic imagery and the world he discards in imperial imagery; it is not insignificant that empire is dwarfed by the cosmos in the comparison.

The fate Octavius has in store for Cleopatra—being led caged through the streets of Rome—symbolizes the conquest of a nation in the conquest of a single female body. Imperialistic constructions of cultural other and patriarchal constructions of sexual other conflate: the conquest of Egypt is emblematized in sexual terms as an Ovidian fantasy—the complete domination of a woman:

> Now, Iras, what think'st thou?
> Thou, an Egyptian puppet, shall be shown
> In Rome as well as I. Mechanic slaves
> With greasy aprons, rules, and hammers shall
> Uplift us to the view. In their thick breaths,
> Rank of gross diet, shall we be enclouded,
> And forc'd to drink their vapor. . . .
>   Saucy lictors
> Will catch at us like strumpets, and scald rhymers
> Ballad 's out a' tune. The quick comedians
> Extemporally will stage us, and present
> Our Alexiandrian revels: Antony
> Shall be brought drunken forth, and I shall see
> Some squeaking Cleopatra boy my greatness
> I' th' posture of a whore.
>
>   (5.2.207–21)

Those who believe that Cleopatra dallies with Octavius out of a desire to strike a bargain with him ignore in her speeches her repeated, explicit preference of death to anything he offers her:

> Not th' imperious show
> Of the full-fortun'd Caesar ever shall
> Be brooch'd with me, if knife, drugs, serpents have
> Edge, sting, or operation.
>
> (4.15.23–26)

> 'Tis paltry to be Caesar;
> Not being Fortune, he's but Fortune's knave,
> A minister of her will: and it is great
> To do that thing that ends all other deeds,
> Which shackles accidents and bolts up change,
> Which sleeps, and never palates more the dung.
>
> (5.2.2–7)

> Know, sir, that I
> Will not wait pinion'd at your master's court. . . .
> Rather a ditch in Egypt
> Be gentle grave unto me! rather on Nilus' mud
> Lay me stark-nak'd, and let the water-flies
> Blow me into abhorring! rather make
> My country's high pyramides my gibbet,
> And hang me up in chains!
>
> (5.2.52–62)

Here, as always, Cleopatra is fully aware of Octavius's imperialistic ideology, its implications for women and for Egypt, and more particularly, the imperatives by which he would reduce her to the most precious of prizes. Likewise, those who interpret her evasion of the fate Octavius has in store for her as motivated by female vanity ignore Antony's identical sentiments:

> Eros,
> Wouldst thou be window'd in great Rome and see
> Thy master thus with pleach'd arms, bending down
> His corrigible neck, his face subdu'd
> To penetrative shame, whilst the wheel'd seat
> Of fortunate Caesar, drawn before him, branded
> His baseness that ensued?
>
> (4.14.71–77)

If the desire to avoid humiliation plays a part in motivating Cleopatra to take her life, then the same must be admitted of Antony.

Far from depicting Cleopatra as overcome by self-interest, vacillating in her determination to die as she seriously entertains Octavius's lies, Shakespeare emphasizes her resolution. Like Antony, she comes to terms with the fear of death to take her life. From the moment of his death to that of her own she invokes the courage needed to perform the final deed:

> My resolution and my hands I'll trust,
> None about Caesar.
>
> (4.15.49–50)

> Come, we have no friend
> But resolution and the briefest end.
>
> (4.15.90–91)

> My resolution's plac'd, and I have nothing
> Of woman in me. . . .
>
> (5.2.238–39)

> Husband, I come!
> Now to that name my courage prove my title!
>
> (5.2.287–88)

The richly comic exchange in which she exploits and manipulates Octavius's belief in female "frailty" further discloses her resolution. Her strategy of dissembling with the "sole sir o' th' world" guarantees the success of her practical joke: "I . . . do confess I have / Been laden with like frailties which before / Have often sham'd our sex" (5.2.121–24).

The pleasure Cleopatra takes in outfoxing Octavius at his own game dominates the final moments of the play: "Why, that's the way / To fool their preparation, and to conquer / Their most absurd intents" (5.2.224–26). Twice she underscores her success. Of Antony she exults, "I hear him mock / The luck of Caesar" (5.2.285–86). To the asp she laughs, "O, couldst thou speak, / That I might hear thee call great Caesar ass / Unpolicied!" (5.2.306–8). Four more times the text insists upon her success. Nearly every character on stage—Charmian, the First Guard, Dolabella, and Octavius himself—accentuates Cleopatra's victory and Octavius's defeat in this final battle of wills and wits:

> *Charmian.* Now boast thee, death, in thy possession lies
>   A lass unparallel'd.
>
> (5.2.315–16)

> *1. Guard.*   . . . all's not well; Caesar's beguil'd.
>
> (5.2.323)

> *Dolabella.*   Caesar, . . .
>   thyself art coming
> To see perform'd the dreaded act which thou
> So sought'st to hinder. . . .
> That you did fear is done.
>
> (5.2.329–35)

> *Caesar.* She levell'd at our purposes, and being royal
> Took her own way.
>
> (5.2.336–37)

Cleopatra transforms the humiliating procession of Octavius intends
for her in Rome into the final procession of her intent: the final
theatrical emblem is that of Octavius bearing her dead body off stage.

As self-aggrandizing at the end of act 5 as at the beginning ("her life
in Rome / Would be eternal in our triumph"), Octavius proclaims the
heroism of the lovers' story only to glorify his own role in it:

>   High events as these
> Strike those that make them; and their story is
> No less in pity than his glory which
> Brought them to be lamented.
>
> (5.2.360–63)

A Roman is as great, in other words, as those he degrades. Octavius's
"place i' th' story" of Antony and Cleopatra, as we well know,
however, is but a footnote. Despite Antony's humiliation and defeat
at Octavius's hands, Cleopatra subverts Octavius's attempt to reduce
her "infinite variety" to the status of a war trophy. The final impression of affirmation and triumph, release and joy, lies in the one more
opportunity granted Antony—one that reiterates the reconciliation of
Lear to Cordelia and anticipates the second chance granted such
protagonists as Leontes in the romances. And it lies in the success of
Cleopatra's practical joke on "the universal landlord" as she enacts a
marital union to Antony.

Time and again she emphasizes the nobility of joining him: "what's
brave, what's noble, / Let's do 't after the high Roman fashion, / And
make death proud to take us" (4.15.86–88). Throughout the final
scene she insists on the nobility of her death:

> He words me, girls, he words me, that I should not
> Be noble to myself.
>
> (5.2.191–92)

                     What poor an instrument
          May do a noble deed!

                                                        (5.2.236–37)

                     Methinks I hear
          Antony call; I see him rouse himself
          To praise my noble act.

                                                        (5.2.283–85)

She obviously does not yearn to emulate Octavius's Rome, as some
critics believe. Instead, her death surpasses the phallic standard of
Roman suicide, as Goldman insists. Her death is "no terse, stoic
acceptance of a sword in the belly"; rather, it is "a conversion of death
into something gentle, regenerative,[30] sovereign" (1985, 132). Indeed,
the final orchestrated spectacle of her death—the fullest manifestation
in the play of the power of her imaginative command—is all of these
things. Its theatrical power lies, to a large extent, in its expression of
the multiplicity of her nature: she is at once wife, queen, mother,
goddess. Her singular aim is to join Antony: "Husband, I come!"
(5.2.287). The final tableau—regal queen seated on her throne—
deliberately recalls the choreographed majesty of their meeting: "I am
again for Cydnus / To meet Mark Antony" (5.2.228–29). Yet the
peaceful, intimate atmosphere that pervades the scene as she nurses
the asps at her breast suggests all domestic scenes of maternal bliss.
Finally, Cleopatra is "serpent of old Nile," theatrically emblematizing
the figure of a prepatriarchal goddess entwined with snakes.[31]
   Shakespeare's representation of Cleopatra humanizes her, disrupt-
ing centuries of treatment of the legend of the two lovers. In *Antony
and Cleopatra* women are most emphatically *not* as they are valued by
men. More so than is true of any of Shakespeare's female protagonists, Cleopatra's estimation of herself is independent of male
estimations of her. She forever eludes and defies delimiting Roman
constructions of her and Egypt—Petrarchism, Ovidianism, and Orientalism. It is Cleopatra's theatrical subjectivity—the complete independence of her self-evaluation from their conflicting desire and
repugnance for her—that accounts for her "infinite variety."
Cleopatra is, literally, more than they can comprehend. She is an
artist who "fashions out of her life a legend that is unfit for hearse or
for Octavius' half-acre tombs." She dies instead seated on the throne
of Egypt, and like the Isis of Egyptian iconography, she represents
that throne. Her "place i' th' story" is beside the legendary figures
who live in ancient myth. She is "another Thetis, an Isis, a Venus, a
Dido," Ornstein concludes ([1966] 1967, 402–3). Indeed, Shake-

speare's treatment of the legend of Cleopatra and Antony is richly reminiscent of the legend of Isis and Osiris, the prime myth of the goddess as redeemer from the prepatriarchal period. The goddess Isis—or Cleopatra—goes in quest of her lost lover Osiris—or Antony—and through her loyalty and descent into the realm of death—Octavius's Rome—recovers him. In Shakespeare's final representation in the love tragedies of the woman as regenerator, Cleopatra is a manifestation of a prepatriarchal goddess.

5

Human Affiliation and the Wedge of Gender

Only connect . . .

—E. M. Forster, *Howards End*

The love tragedies offer Shakespeare the opportunity to explore in gender relationships the paradox of men and women as distinct from one another in their masculinity and femininity, yet connected to one another in their common humanity. And he insists on the common humanity connecting the sexes despite the wedge driven between them by cultural constructions of gender. "The problem appears to be one of construction," as psychoanalyst Carol Gilligan puts it, "an issue of judgment rather than truth" (1982, 171). To be a full human being, Shakespeare intimates, is to be a relational, rather than an autonomous being; yet he gives unblinking attention to the excruciating vulnerability involved in doing so. When he narrows the focus in tragedy to the single, particular heterosexual relationship, rather than the multiple relationships or the general social milieu of comedy, he intensifies his scrutiny of cultural constructions of the masculine and the feminine. The love relationship is the crucible in which Shakespeare tests and examines constructions of masculinity and femininity and discloses the common humanity that eludes and defies those constructions. The emphasis in the tragedies is on the human uniqueness underlying the cultural constructions of gender and, consequently, the disparity—even conflict—between the two.[1]

Shakespeare represents as honorable, heroic, and noble not martial but marital matters, not conventional adventure and conquest, but venturing and questing in matters of the heart. Love depends upon the ability and willingness to give of oneself to another despite the vulnerability of doing so, recalling the message on the lead casket in *The Merchant of Venice*: "Who chooseth me must give and hazard all he hath" (*The Merchant of Venice*, 2.7.9). This emphasis on active generosity in love characterizes the female protagonists of the comedies:

> *Rosalind.* To you I give myself, for I am yours.
>
> (*As You Like It*, 5.4.117)

> *Olivia.* Love sought is good, but given unsought is better.
>
> (*Twelfth Night*, 3.1.156)

> *Helena.* I dare not say I take you, but I give
>   Me and my service, ever whilst I live,
>   Into your guiding power.
>
> (*All's Well That Ends Well*, 2.3.102–4)

In the love tragedies, active generosity is made explicit in Juliet's quintessential expression of her love for Romeo (*Romeo and Juliet*, 2.2.133–35). Juliet, Desdemona, and Cleopatra all generously commit themselves in love; they "give" freely of themselves without hesitation and without qualification. Generosity in love, if we agree with E. M. Forster, is held in a delicate balance with its opposite, expectation: "when human beings love they try to get something. They also try to give something, and this double aim makes love more complicated [than other experiences]. It is selfish and altruistic at the same time," he says; "it is this emotional communion, this desire to give and to get, this mixture of generosity and expectation, that distinguishes love" ([1927] 1985, 50–51). Yet Juliet, Desdemona, and Cleopatra are remarkable in neither expecting nor demanding any "measure for measure" of emotional commitment from their lovers in return. Nor do they weigh and judge any defects or faults of character in the balance. Juliet refuses to blame her husband for killing her cousin, even as Cleopatra refuses to berate Antony for his repeated acts of disloyalty and mistrust. Desdemona's submission to Othello's mistreatment despite her awareness that she is undeserving of it makes the generosity of her forgiveness approach the absoluteness of charity.[2] All three female protagonists love the whole of the other person for that person's sake; they love for the intrinsic value of loving, rather than for any instrumental value.

If love depends upon the ability and willingness to give of oneself to another despite the vulnerability of doing so, Juliet, Desdemona, and Cleopatra "hazard" as well as "give" in love without hesitation and without qualification. The emphasis falls on their confidence in the choice of husband or lover, whether that choice occurs invisibly within the dramatic action, as is true of Juliet,[3] or before the action of the play begins, as is true of Desdemona and Cleopatra. Human beings value and try to balance the competing claims of stability and risk. This balance is never a "tension-free harmony," as political and moral philosopher Martha Nussbaum puts it; it is, rather, "a tension-laden holding-in-focus" (1986, 372). Shakespeare's female protagonists sacrifice stability and balance and embody the willingness to hazard, wager, and risk all: "That I did love the Moor to live with him, / My downright violence, and storm of fortunes, / May trumpet to the world" (*Othello*, 1.3.248–50). The risk they take in love constitutes in part the value of that love.

The fragility of the love between two people lies in its peculiar vulnerability to happenings in the world. Because the odds against intimacy are so great, we wonder that it flourishes at all—in our world as well as in the dramatic worlds of Shakespeare's tragedies. The female protagonists in *Antony and Cleopatra*, *Othello*, and *Romeo and Juliet* share with the speaker in Shakespeare's sonnets the courage to love despite awareness of the vicissitudes of human existence. Desdemona's confidence in her love allows her to rejoice at the prospect of its deepening: "The heavens forbid / But that our loves and comforts should increase, / Even as our days do grow!" (*Othello*, 2.1.195–97). Although she is free of the doubts that haunt Othello, she understands that his expressions of absoluteness of affection, are, perhaps, attempts to protect his love from the unknown that the passage of time brings:

> If it were now to die,
> 'Twere now to be most happy; for I fear
> My soul hath her content so absolute
> That not another comfort like to this
> Succeeds in unknown fate.
>
> (*Othello*, 2.1.189–93)

Whereas Othello, like so many of Shakespeare's male protagonists—and like the speaker in John Donne's *Songs and Sonnets*—is capable of trusting only in the immutable and the stable, Desdemona, like so many of his female protagonists, is capable of the far more difficult thing, trusting in the mutable and the unstable. Her confidence in the face of mutability, as we have seen, is somewhat akin to that of the speaker in Shakespeare's sonnets.[4] Juliet and Cleopatra share this confidence. Cleopatra, further, shares with the speaker in Shakespeare's sonnets the confidence that what she loves will stand against death. In Sonnet 18, for example, the speaker expresses confidence that his love will stand against the ravages of time, although with a deliberateness and self-consciousness about his poetic artistry that is absent in Cleopatra's tribute:

Shall I compare thee to a summer's day?
Thou art more lovely and more temperate:
Rough winds do shake the darling buds of May,
And summer's lease hath all too short a date;
Sometime too hot the eye of heaven shines,
And often is his gold complexion dimm'd,
And every fair from fair sometime declines,
By chance or nature's changing course untrimm'd:
But thy eternal summer shall not fade,
Nor lose possession of that fair thou ow'st,
Nor shall Death brag thou wand'rest in his shade,
When in eternal lines to time thou grow'st.
  So long as men can breathe or eyes can see,
  So long lives this, and this gives life to thee.

It is not coincidental that Antony takes on mythological proportions—"His legs bestrid the ocean; his rear'd arm / Crested the world, his voice was propertied / As all the tuned spheres" (*Antony and Cleopatra*, 5.2.82–84)—when Cleopatra's poetic artistry immortalizes him. Nor is it coincidental that Shakespeare's dramatic artistry includes both death and the confidence in the human capacity for love that stands against death. Cleopatra's poetic imagination, like Shakespeare's dramatic artistry, creates art; art, in turn, shapes future imaginative and cultural impressions. In a very real way, our contemporary sense of who Antony is is the result of Cleopatra's making. In a very real way, our contemporary understanding of the ability to love in the face of human mutability and mortality is that of Shakespeare's making. Literature does more, of course, than mimetically "reflect a context outside itself," as Jean Howard observes; it also constitutes a means of production, or "one of the creative forces of history." Literature is accorded real power when we acknowledge that, rather than "passively reflecting an external reality," it actively participates in "constructing a culture's sense of itself" (1986, 26, 25).

In *Othello*, more so than in any other work, Shakespeare rigorously interrogates the unilateral standards of female chastity and male honor—and the dependency of the latter upon the former—and finds them wanting. The single sonnet which offers an image of ideal love assumes that it depends upon a constancy that is mutual. The opening lines of Sonnet 116 insist that the love that does not "admit impediments" is a "marriage" of "true" minds:

Let me not to the marriage of true minds
Admit impediments; love is not love
Which alters when it alteration finds,
Or bends with the remover to remove.

The sexual relationships in the love tragedies suggest that love likewise depends for its existence upon a constancy that is mutual. As the
dramatic action of the romantic comedies and the early action of the
love tragedies discloses, two lovers must be able to establish trust in
one another. They must be able to receive one another's love without
suspicion, jealousy, or fear. The foundation of the love and the
continuing trust in that foundation, as the dramatic action of *Othello*
most painfully discloses, must remain constant or the love will be
undermined. Because *Othello* dramatizes the disintegration of the
male protagonist, the emphasis falls on mutual constancy that is
destroyed. Because *Romeo and Juliet* and *Antony and Cleopatra*
dramatize the ennoblement of the male protagonist, the emphasis falls
on mutual constancy that is produced or reproduced.

The ravages of human love, which so often "with base infection"
meet, never reach the "star" of absolute constancy. Absolute constancy exists instead as an ideal, "an ever-fixed mark" by which to
gauge the tempests of sexual relations:

O no, it is an ever-fixed mark
That looks on tempests and is never shaken;
It is the star to every wand'ring bark,
Whose worth's unknown, although his highth be taken.

That is not to say that the female protagonists in the love tragedies are
heroic in the depth and totality of their emotional commitment, and
the male protagonists are less than heroic in their lack of a like
commitment. Shakespeare depicts both constancy and inconstancy in
the romantic comedies, the sonnets, and the romances, but nowhere
more so than in the love tragedies, I think, does he force upon us the
disparity between the two.

Love and friendship are distinct from other human traits or virtues
in their being not states of being or activities, but in their very nature,
relationships between separate individuals.[5] Being loving or being
friendly is not a state of character, such as the state of being courageous, for example, awaiting an appropriate opportunity, such as the
battlefield, to reveal itself. Just as generosity involves another person,
who must be there to receive, love involves another person, who
must be there to be loved. The other person is significant, moreover,

not merely as an object who receives the activity of giving or love, but as "an intrinsic part of love itself," as Nussbaum puts it, who actively gives or loves in return. Love and friendship are deeply relational—and therefore more vulnerable—because the particular nature of the other "enters more deeply" into defining the particular nature of the relationship (1986, 344).

Mutuality in affection depends not only upon connectedness but also separateness and a mutual respect for that separateness. The other needs to be recognized not as a possession, an extension, or a projection of the self, but as a separate, independent human being whose separateness and independence are valued for their own sakes—for their intrinsic rather than their instrumental value (Nussbaum 1986, 355). The uniqueness of Shakespeare's representation of sexual relationships is his creation of females who are independent, yet relational, human beings. Juliet, Desdemona, and Cleopatra are all endowed with a self-estimation that is independent of the estimations of the men in their dramatic worlds; perhaps it is this singular characteristic—their theatrical subjectivity—that accounts for the fascination that they, and Shakespeare's other female protagonists, hold for audiences and readers over a period of four hundred years. Shakespeare takes pains to convey this sense of independence in the opening action of each play. Yet, having established them as independent rather than clinging figures, he further endows them with a relational, affiliative capacity that the male protagonists often lack.[6] One of the many remarkable things about Cleopatra is that she is a political being, Queen of Egypt, yet, at the same time, devoted to Antony. Men, of course, have "deep yearnings for affiliation," as Miller points out. These needs exist in men as well as women, "deep *under the surface* of social appearance," or cultural constructions of gender. Men, like women, long for "an affiliative mode of living," of course, but have deprived themselves of it for so long that they have made themselves unable to believe in it ([1976] 1986, 87–88). Shakespeare's females, like the contemporary women in Carol Gilligan's study, "replace the bias of men toward separation with a representation of the interdependence of self and other." Also, like the women in Gilligan's study, their sense of integrity is interpenetrated with "an ethic of care"—to see themselves as women is "to see themselves in a relationship of connection" (1982, 170, 171).

Shakespeare's comprehension of human complexity is equaled by his artistry, by his ability to transmute this understanding into the richness and diversity of particular characters in action. This understanding represents as supreme not structures of cultural, religious, military, or political power, but the emotional commitment of personal relationships among family, friends, and lovers. Even as we come to understand this implicit truth manifest in work after work across all genres, so we come to appreciate an artistry that simultaneously uses and breaks literary tradition, that exploits and criticizes in tragedy as in comedy cultural constructions of masculinity and femininity. It presents romantic and antiromantic discursive practices only to expose their inadequacy and to frame an authentic emotional commitment that is rooted in psychological reality. Romeo sheds chivalric roles in his deepening connection to Juliet; Othello falls prey to Iago's misogyny despite his connection to Desdemona; Antony oscillates between Petrarchist, Ovidian, and Orientalist constructions of Cleopatra in his incipient understanding of her "infinite variety."

Shakespeare's female protagonists are remarkable for their totality of being that eludes and defies, disrupts and subverts male constructions of the female. This is nowhere more evident in the canon or, perhaps, in all of western tradition, than in his characterization of Cleopatra. Yet as early as a crossdressed Viola, Shakespeare stresses not patriarchal constructions of femininity but, rather, human traits—sturdiness, sweetness, wittiness, melancholy, resilience—that surpass constructions of either gender. When Shakespeare does decide to endow his females with stereotypically feminine traits—the obedience of Juliet and Desdemona; the chastity of Desdemona; the fear of Juliet and Cleopatra; the devotion of all three female protagonists—it is to evaluate not them, but rather, men and the constructions of woman that operate so powerfully in the dramatic worlds of the plays. Juliet, Desdemona, and Cleopatra recognize and appreciate their lovers' totality of being; this recognition and appreciation, as the dramatic action of play after play discloses, demands reciprocity. For the value of all of Shakespeare's protagonists lies in their human traits, the capacity for love—its generosity, its confidence, its constancy, and its mutuality—supreme among them. Our own understanding of the comprehensiveness of Shakespeare's view of humanity depends upon our understanding of the complexity of his females, as of his males.

Notes

Chapter 1. Intersections of Genre and Gender in Shakespeare's Love Tragedies

1. I find Karen Newman's differentiation between *reflection* and *representation* useful in understanding the mutually constitutive nonmimetic relationship between art and culture:

> Social historians such as Lawrence Stone, as well as political treatises, homilies, and myriad other primary sources, have demonstrated the patriarchal nature of Elizabethan society; Shakespeare's plays represent many of that society's institutions and assumptions. But to conclude from these historical and contextual facts that Shakespeare is somehow lost or diminished for us is to assume that literature *reflects* reality. To read a Shakespeare play as an allegory of 'man's estate' in which women function as a psychological locus of anxiety in the struggle toward identity or to see his powerful comic heroines as subsumed by their erotic plots of courtship and marriage is to see Shakespeare's theater as primarily mimetic. Such interpretations ignore the acts and effects of *representation*, a fundamental category in any literary analysis and one that is particularly useful to a feminist literary criticism. (1984–85, 601–2)

See also nn. 4 and 14.

2. I am adapting the terms *autonomous* and *relational* from Jean Baker Miller ([1976] 1986) and Carol Gilligan (1982).

Both Brodwin (1971, 44–64, 197–254) and Roger Stilling (1976, 67–81, 145–65, 277–89) include Shakespeare in their critical surveys of Elizabethan and Jacobean love tragedies. Brodwin classifies *Romeo and Juliet* as a "tragedy of courtly love," and *Othello* and *Antony and Cleopatra* as two different patterns of "tragedies of worldly love." If she formulates different categories of plays, Stilling seeks the connections among them. He puts forth the notion of "love tragedy" as a genre—characterized by its concern with "the love-death opposition"—which he traces from *Gismond of Salern* in 1560 through John Ford's tragedies in the 1630s. Franklin Dickey (1957), H. A. Mason (1970), and Derick R. C. Marsh (1976) offer book-length studies that examine Shakespeare's love tragedies as a group.

3. To differentiate sex from gender, as best as I am able, I use the terms *male* and *female* to distinguish biological difference and the terms *masculine* and *feminine* to distinguish culturally constructed difference.

4. I find useful Edward Said's insistence on *discursive practice* as an active construction—not merely a passive reflection—of reality: "texts can *create* not only knowledge but also the very reality they appear to describe. In time such knowledge and reality produce a tradition, or what Michel Foucault calls a discourse, whose material presence or weight, not the originality of a given author, is really responsible for the texts produced out of it" (1978, 94). See also Jean Howard (1986, 25).

5. I have adopted for my purposes R. A. Shoaf's titular term (1988).

6. Carol Thomas Neely is, as far as I can discern, the first feminist critic to analyze the dichotomous "degradation" and "idealization" of female characters by

male characters within the dramatic illusion of Shakespeare's texts. This she does in *Othello* (1977, 137). Juliet Dusinberre interrogates this dichotomy in the plays of Shakespeare and his contemporaries generally (1975, 137–98).

7. See Janet Adelman's "Male Bonding in Shakespeare's Comedies" (1985) and Peter Erickson's *Patriarchal Structures in Shakespeare's Drama* (1985) for psychoanalytic/feminist discussions of the conflict between male and heterosexual bonding.

8. The term *Orientalism* is Said's. See chap. 4, n. 1.

9. The interaction between art and culture, of course, is not unilateral. The love ethos, as Boone remarks, was also appropriated "in the church's proliferating cults of the Virgin as a 'beloved' " and "in the eroticized cosmographies (conflating the divine creative urge and Eros) that emanated from the Chartres school of theologians" (1987, 37). See also nn. 1 and 4.

10. Or, alternatively, "to be a subject is to be able to speak, to give meaning" (Belsey 1985, x).

11. All citations of Shakespeare's works are from *The Riverside Shakespeare* (1974).

12. See Linda Woodbridge (1987) for a penetrating analysis of the rigid red-and-white color scheme of Renaissance love poetry as part of "a semiotic code visible throughout human history, worldwide."

13. I am using Neely's terms (1978); she, in turn, adapts these terms from historians Joan Kelly-Gadol and Gerda Lerner (1976). Neely discerns three modes, or phases, of feminist criticism of Shakespeare: "compensatory" critics emphasize the female protagonists, attempting to restore to them their virtues and their central positions; "justificatory" critics examine patriarchal structures in accounting for the limitations of female characters and the male characters' delimiting conceptions of them; "transformational" critics interrogate the boundary between the commanding female protagonists and their confining cultures.

14. The view that the marriages of the female protagonists of the comedies constitute a submission to patriarchy on their part originates, as far as I can discern, with Clara Claiborne Park (1980) and culminates in the work of cultural materialists such as Kathleen McLuskie (1985), which further reveals the intervention of materialist/historicist thought upon feminist thought. I find that my views pertaining to this issue are aligned with not only those of Newman (1984–85; see n. 1), but also those of Jean Howard (1986), Lynda Boose (1987), and Carol Thomas Neely (1988), all of whom scrutinize materialist/historicist approaches to Shakespeare and analyze their implications for gender issues in the texts and for feminist approaches to the texts.

Howard, writing from a historicist perspective, historicizes the historicists—usefully pointing out their reading of late-twentieth century uncertainty and anxiety into early modern England—before summarizing the contributions of Louis Montrose and Stephen Greenblatt. Boose highlights similarities and differences among feminists, cultural materialists, and new historicists. She concludes by historicizing American feminists and new historicists, tracing their shared origins in the social and political events of the 1960s but attributing the "optimism" of feminist critics to the empowering effects of the women's liberation movement and the "pessimism" of historicist critics to the emasculating effects of the Vietnam draft. Neely attacks cultural materialists and new historicists, among other theoretical approaches, deliciously elides their labels into the tag, "cult/historicist," and objects to their oppression of women, repression of sexuality, subordination of gender issues, and denial of unity, autonomy, and identity in authors, subjects, and texts. See also McLuskie's response to Neely (1989, 224–29).

Although it is difficult to map the quickly shifting landscape of contemporary theoretical approaches to Shakespeare, these three feminists not only give a new shape to the contours of recent theoretical debate, they also begin to mark the boundaries of materialist/historicist approaches, at least for feminists.

15. For remarks on Shakespeare's "essential conservatism and phallocentrism," see Carolyn Heilbrun (1982–83, 185). For theories that reinforce rather than deconstruct traditional divisions and definitions, see Marilyn French's introductory chapters on "The Gender Principles" (1981) and Linda Bamber's introductory chapter, "Comic Women, Tragic Men," on "the Self" as masculine and "the Other" as feminine (1982). For disagreement with critics who "reimpose the prescriptions they mean to erase by restating the oppressive categories that must be seen through and must be read beyond for a genuine feminist discourse to arise," see Jonathan Goldberg (1985, 118).

16. I find Teresa de Lauretis's views on subjectivity useful in understanding the reorientation of perspective on the part of the male protagonists. Subjectivity is "an ongoing construction, not a fixed point of departure or arrival from which one then interacts with the world," she maintains. It is an effect of that interaction and thus it is "produced not by external ideas, values, or material causes, but by one's personal, subjective engagement in the practices, discourses, and institutions that lend significance (value, meaning, and affect) to the events of the world" (1984, 159).

Chapter 2. *Romeo and Juliet:* Female Subjectivity and the Petrarchan Discursive Tradition

1. Caroline Spurgeon's early works on imagery reveal the prevalence of light and dark imagery in the play. Lysander's description of true love, "Swift as a shadow, short as any dream, / Brief as the lightning in the collied night" (*A Midsummer Night's Dream*, 1.1.144–45), quintessentially sums up for her the precariousness of the protagonists' love (1930; 1935, 309–16). D. A. Traversi further develops this approach to the play ([1956] 1969, 1:110–39). For Peter Alexander, *Romeo and Juliet*, together with *Richard II, Dream,* and *Merchant,* is "the most poetical" of all the plays because its verse attains "a rare lyrical intensity" (1961, 102–3). Other studies of language not confined to imagery include Molly Mahood (1957, 56–72); Harry Levin ([1960] 1970); Robert O. Evans (1966); Nicholas Brooke (1968, 80–106); Rosalie Colie (1974, 135–46); and Jill Levenson (1982).

2. Gervinus originates the view of Friar Lawrence as a choral character and asserts that "excess in any enjoyment, however pure in itself, transforms sweet into bitterness" ([1850] 1892, 211); John Masefield labels the lovers' passion as "the storm in the blood" (1911, 69); Donald Stauffer claims that "the dangerous fault of the two lovers is their extreme rashness" ([1949] 1964, 30); for Brents Stirling, Friar Lawrence's "Wisely and slow; they stumble that run fast" is the play's theme (1956, 10–25); Franklin Dickey gathers sixteen pages of evidence against Romeo and asserts that "his impetuous nature leads him to despair and die" (1957, 63–117); for Virgil Whitaker, Friar Lawrence's opposition between "grace" and "rude will" sums up the central conflict (1965, 109–119).

3. Edward Dowden disagrees with Gervinus: "Shakspere did not believe that the highest wisdom of human life was acquirable by mild, monastic meditation, and by gathering simples in the coolness of dawn. Friar Lawrence too, old man, had his lesson to learn" (1880, 109). Franz Boas follows Dowden in claiming the protagonists have no consequential faults, but further claims that fate determines the tragic outcome (1896, 206). Later proponents of this view include H. B. Charlton (1939; 1948); William Allan Neilson and Charles Jarvis Hill (1942, 974–75); Harley

Granville-Barker ([1947] 1975, 2:300–49); G. I. Duthie (1955); Geoffrey Bullough (1957, 1:276–83); and Brooke (1968).

4. Those who espouse this view include G. B. Harrison ([1951] 1964, 47–64); Duthie; Dickey; Harold Wilson (1957, 19–31); and Irving Ribner (1959). Charlton, however, debunks the feud, providing a corrective to the providential view.

My most recent experience of *Romeo and Juliet* in the theater—the 1989 Shakespeare/Santa Cruz production—bears out the irrelevance of the providential view. During the one hundred forty lines that follow the deaths of the lovers, the audience is not even listening. Rather, they are staring at the two fresh corpses in the Capulet vault. All that matters is that Romeo and Juliet are dead. In this production's staging of the closing scenes, Juliet's body remained on the upper stage, spotlit, dominating the surrounding action from the close of the potion scene (4.3), throughout 4.4, the lamentations scene (4.5), 5.1, 5.2, and the first half of the vault scene (5.3). Characters in the lamentations scene transformed the wedding bed into a crypt. After Romeo's death both bodies dominated the stage throughout the last one hundred forty lines of 5.3. The theatrical effect that was gained by such a dramaturgical decision was rich and complex, far more so than merely emblematizing the light and dark imagery in the language of the play. It emphasized, instead, the deaths of the lovers and de-emphasized the restitution of social harmony so cherished by the divine providence critics of the 1950s. All of the other characters, in fact, were literally in the dark during 5.3. This decision—like "the tragic loading of this bed" in *Othello*—emphasized the visual image of the bodies of the lovers locked in the dead embrace of the tomb as against that of the lovers locked in the living embrace of their wedding bed in 3.5. Powerfully lodged in the final image of the lovers' destruction, then, was the image of their potentiality, the earlier stage image showing through the final one.

5. The opening dramatic action of *Othello*, like that of *Romeo and Juliet*, features elements of Shakespearean comedy. But immediately the mood is different, darker: not love generally but that of the protagonists themselves is the subject of attack; the cynical mind that reduces love to lust is racist as well. Our first impression of Desdemona's and Othello's love is like that of the dimly comprehending Brabantio, pelted with obscenities in the middle of the night (*Othello*, 1.1.88–117). Philo's attack on the lovers' relationship in the opening lines of *Antony and Cleopatra* (*Antony and Cleopatra*, 1.1.1–13) is not as obscene as Iago's attack on Othello and Desdemona, but is more direct; see chap. 4.

6. See Levenson for an exhaustive catalog and analysis of Petrarchan topoi throughout the play, beginning in this scene and continuing in 2.3, 3.5, 4.1, 4.5, 5.1, and 5.3.

7. Marianne Novy observes that Petrarchism is a structure of feeling as well as a poetic tradition. Both the lover's blazon and introspection "could be written indefinitely without portraying any interaction between the two parties." She writes, "if . . . Petrarchan love poetry flourishes in the absence of mutuality, a Petrarchizing imagination . . . may make mutuality more difficult" (1984, 28).

8. Cf. Lady Capulet's set piece on loving by the book, "This precious book of love, this unbound lover, / To beautify him, only lacks a cover" (1.3.85–86), and Mercutio's mockery of Tybalt for fighting by the book: "O, he's the courageous captain of compliments. He fights as you sing prick-song, keeps time, distance, and proportion . . . a duelist, a duelist; a gentleman of the very first house, of the first and second cause" (2.4.19–25); "a villain, that fights by the book of arithmetic!" (3.1.101–2).

9. Michael Goldman makes the point that Shakespeare "presides over the change

of the word 'self' from a purely grammatical indicator to something like the complex term it is today" (1972, 25). See also his Appendix A, " 'Self' in Shakespeare and the *OED*" (153–58).

10. Erich Fromm describes faith as "a conviction which is rooted in one's own experience of thought or feeling." It is not primarily belief in something, but rather, "the quality of certainty and firmness which our convictions have" (1956, 121).

11. The term is Fromm's, in his discussion of "concentration" as an aspect of the practice of loving: "two people talk in clichés when their hearts are not in what they are saying." Speakers are not genuine in "trivial" conversation, he maintains, whereas they experience what they are talking about in "relevant" conversation (113).

12. Desdemona's and Othello's meeting is not presented on stage; Othello reveals her initiation of courtship: "She . . . bade me, if I had a friend that lov'd her, / I should but teach him how to tell my story, / And that would woo her" (*Othello*, 1.3.163–66). Nor is Cleopatra's and Antony's meeting presented on stage; Enobarbus reveals in the initiation and reciprocation of their dinner invitations the rhythm of mutual attraction and counterattraction that characterizes their relationship from the beginning: "Antony sent to her, / Invited her to supper. She replied, / It should be better he became her guest" (*Antony and Cleopatra*, 2.2.219–21).

13. See G. McGown for an analysis of the conventions of the epithalamium (1976).

14. Many medieval romances illustrate, Boone notes, that the service of love was easily deflected into heroic or national action. "Political enemies as well as dragons," he writes, "could be overwhelmed in the name of one's lady" (1987, 37). See de Rougemont for a discussion of chivalry as the governing principle of both love and war ([1940] 1983, 241–48). See Thompson for an analysis of the conflicting codes of love and honor in *Romeo and Juliet* (1971, 71–76).

15. I am indebted to Harvey Berenberg for the view of the feud as a rite of passage. Among Shakespearean critics, Coppélia Kahn is notable for labeling the feud as a "deadly *rite de passage* that promotes masculinity at the price of life" (1981, 82–103).

16. Franco Zeffirelli's cinematic version of the play indulges in street fighting choreography at the expense of Shakespeare's dialogue, but it also conveys, masterfully, the feud's volatility. Apparently harmless juvenile competitiveness repeatedly escalates, upon the slightest provocation, from exchanges of insults to exchanges of blows.

17. Thomas Moisan (1983) analyzes Shakespeare's use of "artificial" language to convey insincere or shallow emotion on the part of the Nurse, Lady Capulet, Capulet, and Paris upon their discovery of Juliet's "body" in what he calls the "lamentations" scene (4.5).

18. "O, she doth teach the torches to burn bright!"; "But soft, what light through yonder window breaks?"; and so on.

Chapter 3. *Othello*: Female Subjectivity and the Ovidian Discursive Tradition

1. Coleridge ([1960] 1963, 1:205–7); A. C. Bradley ([1904] 1955, 144–96); G. Wilson Knight ([1930] 1957, 97–119); Harley Granville-Barker ([1947] 1975, 2:3–149); and Helen Gardner (1955).

2. T. S. Eliot ([1932] 1968); F. R. Leavis ([1952] 1966); Arthur Kirschbaum (1962, 145–58); William Empson ([1951] 1968); H. A. Mason (1970, 59–161).

3. Robert Heilman points out Desdemona's "progress from infatuated girl toward devoted, enduring wife" (1956, 213). This kind of reading of her character has been the exception rather than the rule. More recently, S. N. [Shirley Nelson] Garner

offers a perspective midway between idealization and disparagement (1976) while Ann Jennulie Cook sees in Desdemona's characterization a pattern that is the inverse of mine (1980). See "The Female Perspective" section and n. 11 of this chap.

4. Heilman's essay, "Wit and Witchcraft: An Approach to *Othello*" ([1956] 1967), is a slightly expanded version of chap. 7 of his book, *Magic in the Web* (1956, 219–29).

5. Gardner reiterates this emphasis, observing that "the tragic experience with which this play is concerned is the loss of faith" (1955, 197); in turn, Norman Rabkin echoes Gardner (1967, 57–79).

6. However, as a recent paper by Robert Bennett demonstrates (1988), the critical attack on the secrecy of the marriage—prevalent among the moralistic readings of the old historicists in the 1950s—has not died. The major flaw of this argument lies in its exceeding degree of tone deafness to the sentiments expressed by the protagonists. Perhaps Bennett, like Dickey before him, would also condemn Romeo and Juliet to their deaths for their "sins" or "crimes" of excessive passion.

7. Indeed, Desdemona's expression of passion for her husband certainly has made critics uncomfortable. The constructions of women and relations between the sexes revealed by the harsh interpretations of her character are identical to those that Shakespeare calls into question with such regularity throughout his works.

8. Donne's "Love's Growth" and Shakespeare's Sonnet 115 best exemplify the difference:

I scarce beleeve my love to be so pure
    As I had thought it was,
    Because it doth endure
Vicissitude, and season, as the grasse;
Me thinkes I lyed all winter, when I swore,
My love was infinite, if spring make' it more.

But if this medicine, love, which cures all sorrow
With more, not onely bee no quintessence,
But mixt of all stuffes, paining soule, or sense,
And of the Sunne his working vigour borrow,
Love's not so pure, and abstract, as they use
To say, which have no Mistresse but their Muse,
But as all else, being elemented too,
Love sometimes would contemplate, sometimes do.

And yet no greater, but more eminent,
    Love by the spring is growne;
    As, in the firmament,
Starres by the Sunne are not inlarg'd, but showne.
Gentle love deeds, as blossomes on a bough,
From loves awakened root do bud out now.

If, as in water stir'd more circles bee
Produc'd by one, love such additions take,
Those like so many spheares, but one heaven make,
For, they are all concentrique unto thee;
And though each spring doe adde to love new heate,
As princes doe in times of action get
New taxes, and remit them not in peace,
No winter shall abate the springs encrease.

The speaker in Sonnet 115, like Desdemona, expresses joy in the deepening of his love despite awareness of the mutability of existence and love:

Those lines that I before have writ do lie,
Even those that said I could not love you dearer,
Yet then my judgment knew no reason why
My most full flame should afterwards burn clearer.
But reckoning Time, whose million'd accidents
Creep in 'twixt vows and change decrees of kings,
Tan sacred beauty, blunt the sharp'st intents,
Divert strong minds to th' course of alt'ring things:
Alas, why, fearing of Time's tyranny,
Might I not then say, "Now I love you best,"
When I was certain o'er incertainty,
Crowning the present, doubting of the rest?
   Love is a babe, then might I not say so,
   To give full growth to that which still doth grow.

9. *OED*, compact ed., s.v. *marriage* and *marry*, and *Oxford Latin Dictionary*, combined ed., s.v. *maritus* and *mas*. See n. 16.

10. For the understanding of military psychology in this and the following paragraph I am indebted to the views of Gwynne Dyer (1985).

11. This, I believe, is the central question concerning Desdemona's characterization. My attempt at an answer, incidentally, takes me on a path that is the inverse of the one followed by Cook (1980). She has profound doubts about Desdemona's actions early in the play—her "disobedience" to her father, for example—that are resolved only as the tragic action develops. I find in these same actions the very traits that we so admire in Shakespeare's comic female protagonists—independence, confidence, the courage to take risks—and I am concerned to understand how and why these traits diminish as the dramatic action turns from comic to tragic.

12. G. Bonnard (1949), I believe, initiates this curious approach; Robert Dickes (1970) continues it.

13. Shakespeare's differing generic representations of women have, of course, drawn the attention of feminist critics. The variety and the vigor of their responses to the gender/genre question is, I believe, an indication of its complexity.

14. The studies of Garner (1976) and Carol Thomas Neely (1977) are notable for emphasizing the links among the three female characters in the tragedy.

15. Kay Stanton reminds us, however, that it was not until Nicholas Rowe's edition that the practice of giving Bianca the designation of "Courtesan" in the *dramatis personae* began (1987, 11).

16. *OED*, compact ed., s.vv. *conjugal, conjugality, marriage*, and *marry* and *Oxford Latin Dictionary*, combined ed., s.vv. *coniugo*, etc., *maritus*, and *mas*: *coniugo* "to join in marriage; to form (a friendship)"; *coniunctio* "the act of joining together, uniting; that state of being joined, union; a bond (of association, friendship, etc., between persons); mutual association, friendship, familiarity; an association by marriage or betrothal, connexion; (also) the entering into such an association"; *coniunctus* "closely associated (by friendship, obligation, kinship, etc.), attached; (of relationships, etc.) close"; *coniungo* "to join together, connect; to yoke together; to unite sexually; to bring into close association, unite (by friendship, obligation, kinship, etc.); to bring into alliance; to form an alliance, make common cause; to join in marriage; to be married"; *maritus* "a husband"; *mas* "male, masculine; possessing masculine faculties or characteristics; manly, virile; the male of the species."

I have adopted the terms *partnership model* and *dominator model* from Riane Eisler (1987, xvii).

Chapter 4. *Antony and Cleopatra*: Female Subjectivity and Orientalism

1. I find Edward Said's *Orientalism* useful in understanding Roman views of Egypt in the play. *Orientalism* is the word he uses to describe the construction of a colonized other, such as the Middle East, by an imperialistic culture, such as England, France, or the United States, to legitimate its own superiority. See, especially, his Introduction (1978, 1–28).

2. L. L. Schücking, in a "realistic" interpretation of Cleopatra's "double" character, reconciles the early wanton and the later tragic queen by posing the notion of her transformation (1922, 119–41); E. E. Stoll, reacting against "sentimental" views of Cleopatra, judges plot to be more important than character ([1930] 1958, 3–29); Stirling sees the play as a satire that denies the lovers' nobility (1956, 157–206); Dickey uses the same historical approach he uses with *Romeo and Juliet* to find a moral lesson in the excesses of passion (1957, 144–202); Whitaker follows Schücking in discovering a transformed Cleopatra at Antony's death (1965, 276–96); Mason denies any meaning to the love relationship, writing that "the interest aroused by Cleopatra at the end is too ideal" and that "she has ceased to be part and parcel of the real" (1970, 229–76).

3. Bradley believes in a "triumph which is more than reconciliation" ([1909] 1964); Knight sees in the play's "transcendental humanism" Shakespeare's subtlest and greatest play ([1931] 1951, 199–342); John Middleton Murry says we cannot judge the play "as a record of action merely; if we do, its essence escapes our judgement" (1936, 294–318); Harold Goddard makes the point that Cleopatra deceives some readers as well as the Romans in the play as to her determination to die with her "husband" (1950, 2:184–308); John Dover Wilson emphasizes Antony's magnanimity and Cleopatra's glory ([1950] 1973); D. A. Traversi echoes Knight's interpretation that the lovers find not death but life in his view that "death becomes release" ([1956] 1969, 2:212–39).

4. See n. 1. I am indebted to Peter Stallybrass's and Allon White's distinctions between *self* and *other, top* and *bottom, high* and *low,* especially their views on the conflicting attraction and repulsion of the first in each set for the second (1986, 1–26).

5. Anyone familiar with this essay will recognize its influence on this chapter.

6. It is useful to note, in this connection, the kundalini system of psychic centers, or chakras, running up the spine. Early on, Antony would seem to be mired in the lower two centers, seats of the animal instincts for eating and reproduction. Throughout the course of the play he can be seen to evolve to the fourth center, at the level of the heart—seat of compassion and concern for the other rather than the self.

7. See Goldman (1985, 123ff.) and Adelman (1973, 144ff.) on the significance of "imaginative transformation," in the first case, and "becoming," in the second case, in the play.

8. Goldman, Rackin, and Ornstein all emphasize the power of imaginative command in the play.

9. See n. 4.

10. Again, although I do not wish to press the point, the link between this characterizing trait of Octavius and the third psychic center in the kundalini system—the seat of aggressiveness and the desire for dominance and power over others—is striking. See n. 6 above.

11. The similarity of Octavius's generalized sentiments on female "corruptibility"

and those of Iago on female "appetite" links these two inflections of the Ovidian discursive tradition to one another.

12. Cf. Shakespeare's emblematized marriage ceremony when Othello and Iago kneel side by side at the conclusion of 3.3.

13. For a theatrical interpretation that emphasizes Octavius's genuine feeling for his sister, however, see Alan Dessen's review (1988) of the Peter Hall production at the National Theatre.

14. According to recent findings by archaeologists of prepatriarchal cultures, such as Marija Gimbutas, "the female principle was conceived as creative and eternal, the male as spontaneous and ephemeral" (1982 Women 29). I find that this differentiation has striking resemblances to Shakespeare's representation of gender difference.

Among Shakespeareans, see Neely (1985, 138) and Bamber (1982, 59–60) as well as Dusinberre for discussions of this gender difference in *Antony and Cleopatra*. I read Neely's chapter while revising mine for publication; although we arrived at our conclusions independently, our interpretations intersect at points.

15. "Women's *jouissance* carries with it the notion of fluidity, diffusion, duration. It is a kind of potlatch in the world of orgasms, a giving, expending, dispensing of pleasure without concern about ends or closure" (Marks and de Courtivron 1980, 36–37, n. 8). See also Kristeva (1980).

16. I find that my view of Antony's potential is akin to the materialist conception of subjectivity as articulated by Jonathan Dollimore. Insofar as subjectivity "retains the concept of essence," he says, it "construes it not as that which is eternally fixed but as social potential materialising within limiting historical conditions" (1984, 251).

17. The most stunning opening of this play I have seen is that of the 1988 Shakespeare/Santa Cruz production on the University of California campus, in which Cleopatra and Antony enter 1.1 crossdressed in the way Cleopatra describes. Her recollection is thus given material, symbolic weight in being theatrically enacted on stage in this way.

18. I do not mean that Antony takes up Cleopatra's use of a garment metaphor here; my point is that the verb, *ride,* in the sense of "to mount sexually," is conventionally used with a male, not a female subject. See Eric Partridge ([1948] 1969, 175).

19. I am here, as elsewhere, drawing on the work of Stallybrass and White, who, in turn, draw on Mikhail Bakhtin's distinctions between the *classic* and the *grotesque.* See, especially, their Introduction (1986, 1–26); see also Bakhtin (1968).

20. The relational and emotional sterility of Shakespeare's representation of Octavius contrasts, of course, with his representation of the lovers, but it is all the more striking in light of Roman projections of sexuality onto Cleopatra.

21. Cf. Othello's identity crisis—"Othello's occupation's gone" (*Othello,* 3.3.357)—which is prompted by the delusion of Desdemona's adultery.

22. It is difficult to understand how critics find evidence of her betrayal of Antony in her obvious dissembling with Thidias.

23. Indeed, Neely labels this passage Antony's "boldest declaration of passion in the play" (1985, 146).

24. See n. 14.

25. See Goldman's fine discussion of "imaginative command," "vertical promotion," and "enhancement" during Antony's and Cleopatra's final moments (1985, 112–39).

26. I am not unaware of the sarcasm of this sonnet. Indeed, it can be argued that it makes sense only if the lover does not love the speaker, and that the speaker is aware of this fact.

27. Even those critics who revile Cleopatra have not been able to ignore this

passage; instead, they are forced to erect notions of two Cleopatras—one, a whore; the other, a tragic female protagonist. See n. 2. To other critics, those who would deny Cleopatra her subjectivity because "she dies for love," only the obvious can be pointed out: so does Antony. Desdemona dies for love, but so does Othello; Juliet dies for love, but so does Romeo. Perhaps it is more accurate to say that what is under attack here is any or all human affective affiliation, rather than strictly female affective affiliation.

28. See n. 14.

29. L. T. Fitz [Linda Woodbridge] usefully summarizes and analyzes the indifferent, unsympathetic—even hostile—critical responses to Shakespeare's characterization of Cleopatra (1977).

30. It may be true, as the Pelican edition notes, that when the Clown says, "his [the asp's] biting is immortal" (5.2.246), he means *mortal*, not *immortal*, and, further, that Cleopatra playfully takes up his malapropism: "I have / Immortal longings in me" (5.2.280). Consider, though, that the snake was the vehicle of immortality in prepatriarchal iconography, according to Gimbutas. "The involved ornamentation of Cucuteni and East Balkan ceramic painting is a symbolic glorification of nature's dynamism," she notes. "Its graphic expression is organized around the symbol of the snake, whose presence was a guarantee that nature's enigmatic cycle would be maintained and its life-giving powers not diminish" (1982 Goddesses 95).

31. The emblem of Cleopatra seated on her throne applying asps to her body bears striking resemblance to the artifacts of prepatriarchal Europe: "from the Early Neolithic to ancient Greece the snake appears in an anthropomorphic shape as a Snake Goddess," Gimbutas points out. "Her body is usually decorated with stripes or snake spirals, while her arms and legs are portrayed as snakes, or she is entwined by one or more snakes" (1982 Goddesses 101).

Chapter 5. Human Affiliation and the Wedge of Gender

1. I agree with Kate McLuskie's claim that an important part of the feminist project is "to insist that the alternative to the patriarchal family and heterosexual love is not chaos but the possibility of new forms of social organization and affective relationships" (1985, 106). The difference between McLuskie and myself is her refusal to acknowledge the contribution of the artist to such a project. The assumption that the dramatic text mimetically reflects the patriarchal culture in which it is produced seems overly deterministic to me. The assumption that artists participate in the consolidation of the dominant ideology rather than any subversion of it renders them, of course, mere factotums of that order—all exposure, critique, or condemnation of the inequities in the dominant order drained from their texts. See Louis Montrose for a discussion of "the inevitably reductive tendency" toward an "overcompensatory positing of subject as wholly determined by structure" (1986, 9).

2. I am aware of the difficulty of considering the generosity of Shakespeare's female characters as an admirable trait. Because it is a stereotypically feminine trait, some assume it is, therefore, not admirable. This view, again, reveals the intervention of materialist/historicist thought upon feminist thought. In psychotherapy, it is true that, as Jean Baker Miller notes, "women often spend a great deal more time talking about giving than men do." By contrast, the question of whether a man is a giver or giving enough does not enter into his self-image; he is concerned more about doing than giving ([1976] 1986, 50).

3. By invisible I mean that we cannot point to a specific moment in the dramatic action of *Romeo and Juliet*, whether the feast scene or the orchard scene, and say,

"Here, Juliet makes her choice." Rather, her nature is imbued, in the way Fromm describes, with a readiness for emotional commitment that governs all her interactions with Romeo: "Faith is a character trait pervading the whole personality, rather than a specific belief" (1956, 121).

4. See Sonnet 115, chap. 3, n. 8.

5. For the understanding of mutuality in this and the following paragraph, I am indebted to the views of Nussbaum. She is discussing Aristotle's notion of *philia*, which she translates as *love* rather than *friendship* (1986, 354). See her chap. 12, on relational goods and the vulnerability of the good human life (1986, 343–372).

6. The attribution of relational capacities or affiliative modes of living to Shakespeare's female characters leads some critics to conclude that Shakespeare is a "patriarchal bard" (McLuskie 1985; but see also McLuskie 1989, 224–30). The assumption is that his attribution of those human traits which are culturally labeled *feminine* to female characters constitutes his active, if not deliberate, participation in the reproduction of patriarchy. This view, again, reveals the enormous impact of materialist/historicist thought upon feminist thought. Peter Stallybrass, however, concludes a recent interrogation of the problems of connecting analyses of gender to analyses of class with a useful suggestion: "it is important to work with both feminism and marxism," he maintains, "without trying to 'marry' them" (1989). Acting to create female-defined values is a more fruitful endeavor, I believe, then reacting to those of male-dominated approaches. Shaping female-defined discursive practices is, in other words, a more valuable strategy than aping male-dominated discursive practices.

Works Cited

Adelman, J. 1973. *The common liar.* Yale Studies in English, no. 181. New Haven: Yale University Press.

———. 1985. Male bonding in Shakespeare's comedies. In *Shakespeare's "rough magic."* Ed. P. Erickson and C. Kahn. Newark: University of Delaware Press.

Alexander, P. 1961. *Shakespeare's life and art.* New York: New York University Press.

Bakhtin, M. M. 1968. *Rabelais and his world.* Trans. H. Iswolsky. Cambridge: MIT Press.

Bamber, L. 1982. *Comic women, tragic men.* Stanford: Stanford University Press.

Belsey, C. 1985. *The subject of tragedy.* London and New York: Methuen.

———. 1988. The matter of history. Paper read at session, System and Antisystem in the English Renaissance III: Transgression. MLA Convention, 27–30 December, New Orleans.

Bennett, R. 1988. The error of elopement and the confusion of love and war in *Othello.* Paper presented at seminar, *Othello:* New Perspectives. Annual meeting of Shakespeare Assn. of America, 31 March–2 April, Boston.

Boas, F. 1896. *Shakspere and his predecessors.* New York.

Bonnard, G. 1949. Are Othello and Desdemona innocent or guilty? *English Studies* 30:175–84.

Boone, J. A. 1987. *Tradition counter tradition.* Chicago: University of Chicago Press.

Boose, L. 1987. The family in Shakespeare studies; or—studies in the family of Shakespeareans; or—the politics of politics. *Renaissance Quarterly* 40:707–42.

Bradley, A. C. [1904] 1955. *Shakespearean tragedy.* Repr. Cleveland: World.

———. [1909] 1964. Shakespeare's *Antony and Cleopatra.* In *Antony and Cleopatra,* ed. B. Everett, 218–43. New York: NAL. (First published in *Oxford lectures on poetry.* London: Macmillan.)

Brodwin, L. 1971. *Elizabethan love tragedy 1587–1625.* New York: New York University Press.

Bronowski, J. 1973. *The ascent of man.* Boston: Little, Brown.

Brooke, A. [1562] 1957. *The tragicall historye of Romeus and Juliet.* In vol. 1 of *Narrative and dramatic sources of Shakespeare,* 284–363. *See* Bullough 1957–73.

Brooke, N. 1968. *Shakespeare's early tragedies.* London: Methuen.

Bullough, G., ed. 1957–73. *Narrative and dramatic sources of Shakespeare.* 8 vols. London: Routledge; New York: Columbia University Press.

Calderwood, J. [1971] 1984. *Romeo and Juliet.* In *Shakespeare,* ed. R. Heilman, 37–49. Englewood Cliffs, N.J.: Prentice. (First published in *Shakespearean metadrama.* Minneapolis: University of Minnesota Press.)

Campbell, J. 1988. *The power of myth.* New York: Doubleday.

Charlton, H. B. 1939. *Romeo and Juliet* as an experimental tragedy. Proc. of the British Acad. 25:143–85.

———. 1948. *Shakespearian tragedy.* Cambridge: Cambridge University Press.

Cinthio, G. [1566] 1973. *Gli hecatommithi.* Trans. G. Bullough. In vol. 7 of *Narrative and dramatic sources of Shakespeare,* 239–52. *See* Bullough 1957–73.

Cixous, H. 1976. The laugh of the Medusa. Trans. K. Cohen and P. Cohen. *Signs* 1:875–93.

Coleridge, S. T. [1960] 1963. Comments on *Othello.* In *Othello,* ed. A. Kernan, 205–7. New York: NAL. (First published in vol. 1 of *Shakespearean criticism,* ed. T. Raysor. 2nd ed. New York: Dutton.)

———. [1960] 1964. The lectures of 1811–1812, lecture 7. In *Romeo and Juliet,* ed. J. A. Bryant, Jr., 173–83. New York: NAL. (First published in vol. 2 of *Shakespearean criticism,* ed. T. Raysor. 2nd ed. New York: Dutton.)

Colie, R. 1974. *Shakespeare's living art.* Princeton, N.J.: Princeton University Press.

Cook, A. 1980. The design of Desdemona. *Shakespeare Studies* 13:187–96.

Council, N. 1973. *When honour's at the stake.* London: Allen.

Dash, I. 1981. *Wooing, wedding, and power.* New York: Columbia University Press.

Dean, L., ed. 1967. *Shakespeare.* Rev. ed. London: Oxford University Press.

DeLauretis, T. 1984. *Alice doesn't.* Bloomington: Indiana University Press.

Dessen, A. 1988. Exploring the script. *Shakespeare Quarterly* 39:217–26.

Dickes, R. 1970. Desdemona: an innocent victim? *American Imago* 27:279–97.

Dickey, F. 1957. *Not wisely but too well.* San Marino: Huntington Library.

Dollimore, J. 1984. *Radical tragedy.* Chicago: University of Chicago Press.

Donne, J. [1933] 1977. *Poetical works.* Ed. H. Grierson. Repr. Oxford: Oxford University Press.

Doran, M. [1954] 1964. *Endeavors of art.* Repr. Madison: University of Wisconsin Press.

———. 1976. The idea of excellence in Shakespeare. *Shakespeare Quarterly* 27:133–49.

Dowden, E. 1880. *Shakspere.* 3rd ed. New York: Harper.

Dyer, G. 1985. *War.* Chicago: Dorsey.

Dusinberre, J. 1975. *Shakespeare and the nature of women.* New York: Harper.

Duthie, G. 1955. Introd. to *Romeo and Juliet,* ed. J. D. Wilson and Duthie, xi–xxxvii. Cambridge: Cambridge University Press.

Edwards, M., Dir. 1988. *Antony and Cleopatra.* Shakespeare/Santa Cruz.

Eisler, R. 1987. *The chalice and the blade.* San Francisco: Harper.

Eliot, T. S. [1932] 1968. Shakespeare and the stoicism of Seneca. In *Shakespeare's tragedies. See* Lerner 1968, 301–13. (First published in *Selected essays.* New York: Harcourt.)

Empson, W. [1951] 1968. Honest in *Othello.* In *Shakespeare's tragedies. See* Lerner 1968, 106–19. (First published in *The structure of complex words.* London: Chatto.)

Erickson, P. 1985. *Patriarchal structures in Shakespeare's drama.* Berkeley: University of California Press.

Evans, R. 1966. *The osier cage*. Lexington: University of Kentucky Press.

Everett, B. 1964. Introd. to *Antony and Cleopatra*, ed. Everett, xxi–xxxvii. New York: NAL.

Fitz, L. T. [L. Woodbridge]. 1977. Egyptian queens and male reviewers. *Shakespeare Quarterly* 28: 297–316.

Forster, E. M. [1921] 1959. *Howards End*. New York: Vintage.

———. [1927] 1985. *Aspects of the novel*. Repr. New York: Harcourt.

Foucault, M. 1971. Le bibliothèque fantastique. Preface to *La tentation de Saint Antoine*. In vol. 1 of Flaubert's *Oeuvres*, 7–33. Paris: Gallimard.

French, M. 1981. *Shakespeare's division of experience*. New York: Simon.

Fromm, E. 1956. *The art of loving*. New York: Harper.

Frye, N. [1957] 1970. *Anatomy of criticism*. Repr. New York: Atheneum.

Gardner, H. 1955. The noble moor. Proc. of the British Acad. 41: 189–205.

Garner, S. N. 1976. Shakespeare's Desdemona. *Shakespeare Studies* 9: 233–52.

Gervinus, G. [1850] 1892. *Shakespeare commentaries*. Trans. F. E. Beinnett. 5th ed. London.

Gilligan, C. 1982. *In a different voice*. Cambridge and London: Harvard University Press.

Gimbutas, M. 1982. *The goddesses and gods of Old Europe*. Berkeley: University of California Press.

———. 1982. Women and culture in goddess-oriented Old Europe. In *The politics of women's spirituality*, ed. C. Spretnak, 22–31. Garden City: Anchor.

Goddard, H. 1950. *The meaning of Shakespeare*. 2 vols. Chicago: University of Chicago Press.

Goldberg, J. 1985. Shakespearean inscriptions. In *Shakespeare and the question of theory*. See Parker and Hartman 1985, 116–37.

Goldman, M. 1972. *Shakespeare and the energies of drama*. Princeton, N.J.: Princeton University Press.

———. 1985. *Acting and action in Shakespearean tragedy*. Princeton, N.J.: Princeton University Press.

Granville-Barker, H. [1946–47] 1974–75. *Prefaces to Shakespeare*. 2 vols. Repr. Princeton, N.J.: Princeton University Press.

Greene, G. 1979. "This that you call love." *Journal of Women's Studies in Literature* 1:16–32.

Guillaume de Lorris and Jean de Meun. 1962. *The romance of the rose*. Trans. H. W. Robbins. Ed. C. W. Dunn. New York: Dutton.

Harbage, A. 1963. *William Shakespeare*. New York: Farrar.

Harrison, G. B. [1951] 1964. *Shakespeare's tragedies*. Repr. London: Routledge.

Heilbrun, C. 1982–83. Rev. of *The woman's part*, ed. C. Lenz, G. Greene, and C. Neely; *Shakespeare's division of experience*, by M. French; and *Man's estate*, by C. Kahn. *Signs* 8: 182–86.

Heilman, R. 1956. *Magic in the web*. Lexington: University of Kentucky Press.

———. [1956] 1967. Wit and witchcraft. In *Shakespeare. See* Dean 1967, 329–45. (First published in *Sewanee Review* 64:1–10.)

Hibbard, G. 1973. *Titus Andronicus* and *Romeo and Juliet*. In *Shakespeare*, ed. S. Wells, 134–44. London: Oxford University Press.

Howard, J. 1986. The new historicism and Renaissance studies. *English Literary Renaissance* 16:13–43.

Huizinga, J. 1924. *The waning of the middle ages.* Trans. F. Hopman. New York: St. Martin's.

Irigaray, L. 1985. *Speculum of the other woman.* Trans. G. C. Gill. Ithaca and London: Cornell University Press.

Kahn, C. 1981. *Man's estate.* Berkeley: University of California Press.

Kelly-Gadol, J., and G. Lerner. 1976. Notes on women in the Renaissance. In *Conceptual frameworks in women's history.* Bronxville: Sarah Lawrence Publications.

Kermode, F. 1974. Introd. to *Romeo and Juliet, Othello,* and *Antony and Cleopatra.* In *The Riverside Shakespeare. See* Shakespeare 1974, 1055–57, 1198–1202, and 1343–46.

Kernan, A., ed. 1970. *Modern Shakespearean criticism.* New York: Harcourt.

Kirschbaum, L. 1962. *Character and characterization in Shakespeare.* Detroit, Mich.: Wayne State University Press.

Klene, J. 1975. Othello. *Shakespeare Quarterly* 26:139–50.

Knight, G. W. [1930] 1957. *The wheel of fire.* Repr. New York: Meridian.

———. [1931] 1951. *The imperial theme.* Repr. London: Methuen.

Kristeva, J. 1980. *Desire in language.* Oxford: Blackwell.

Leavis, F. R. [1952] 1966. Diabolic intellect and the noble hero. In *The common pursuit,* 136–59. Repr. London: Penguin.

Lenz, C., G. Greene, and C. T. Neely, eds. 1980. *The woman's part.* Urbana: University of Illinois Press.

Lerner, L., ed. 1968. *Shakespeare's tragedies.* London: Penguin.

Levenson, J. 1982. The definition of love. *Shakespeare Studies* 15:21–36.

Levin, H. [1960] 1970. Form and formality in *Romeo and Juliet.* In *Modern Shakespearean criticism. See* Kernan 1970, 279–90. (First published in *Shakespeare Quarterly* 11:3–11.)

Lewis, C. S. [1936] 1958. *The allegory of love.* Repr. New York: Oxford University Press.

Mack, M. [1960] 1970. The Jacobean Shakespeare. In *Modern Shakespeare criticism. See* Kernan 1970, 323–50. (First published in *Jacobean theatre,* ed. J. R. Brown and B. Harris. Stratford-upon-Avon Studies, no. 1. London: Arnold.)

Mahood, M. 1957. *Shakespeare's wordplay.* London: Methuen.

Marcus, L. 1989. Oral comment in seminar, Materialist-Feminist Criticism of Shakespeare. Annual meeting of Shakespeare Assn. of America, 13–15 April, Austin.

Marks, E., and I. de Courtivron, eds. 1980. *New French feminisms.* New York: Schocken.

Marsh, D. 1976. *Passion lends them power.* Manchester: Manchester University Press.

Masefield, J. 1911. *William Shakespeare.* London: William.

Mason, H. 1970. *Shakespeare's tragedies of love.* London: Chatto.

McGown, G. 1976. "Runnawayes eyes" and Juliet's epithalamium. *Shakespeare Quarterly* 37:150–70.

McLuskie, K. 1985. The patriarchal bard. In *Political Shakespeare*, ed. J. Dollimore and A. Sinfield, 88–108. Manchester: Manchester University Press.

———. 1989. *Renaissance dramatists*. Atlantic Highlands: Humanities Press.

Miller, J. B. [1976] 1986. *Toward a new psychology of women*. 2nd ed. Beacon: Boston.

Moisan, T. 1983. Rhetoric and the rehearsal of death. *Shakespeare Quarterly* 34:389–404.

Moore, C. 1989. "Well-divided disposition." Unpublished paper.

Murry, J. M. 1936. *Shakespeare*. New York: Harcourt.

Neely, C. T. 1977. Women and men in *Othello*. *Shakespeare Studies* 10:153–58.

———. 1978. Feminist criticism of Shakespeare. Paper read at special session, Feminist Criticism of Shakespeare. MLA Convention, 27–30 December, New York.

———. 1985. *Broken nuptials in Shakespeare's plays*. New Haven: Yale University Press.

———. 1988. Constructing the subject. *English Literary Renaissance* 18:5–18.

Neilson, W. A., and C. J. Hill. 1942. Introd. to *Romeo and Juliet, Othello,* and *Antony and Cleopatra*. In *The complete plays and poems of William Shakespeare*, ed. Neilson and Hill, 974–75, 1093–95, and 1244–45. Cambridge: Houghton.

Newman, K. 1984–85. Comment on Heilbrun's review of *The woman's part, Shakespeare's division of experience,* and *Man's estate*. *Signs* 10:601–3.

Novy, M. 1984. *Love's argument*. Chapel Hill: University of North Carolina Press.

Nowottny, W. 1951–52. Justice and love in *Othello*. *University of Toronto Quarterly* 21:330–44.

Nussbaum, M. 1986. *The fragility of goodness*. Cambridge: Cambridge University Press.

Nuttall, A. D. 1983. *A new mimesis*. London: Methuen.

Ornstein, R. [1960] 1965. *The moral vision of Jacobean tragedy*. Repr. Madison: University of Wisconsin Press.

———. [1966] 1967. The ethic of the imagination. In *Shakespeare. See* Dean 1967, 389–404. (First published in *Later Shakespeare*, ed. J. R. Brown and B. Harris. Stratford-upon-Avon Studies, No. 8. London: Arnold.)

———. 1972. *A kingdom for a stage*. Cambridge: Harvard University Press.

Ovid. 1957. *The art of love*. Trans. R. Humphries. Bloomington: Indiana University Press.

Park, C. C. 1980. As we like it. In *The woman's part. See* Lenz, Greene, and Neely 1980, 100–16.

Parker, P., and G. Hartman, eds. 1985. *Shakespeare and the question of theory*. New York: Methuen.

Partridge, E. [1948] 1969. *Shakespeare's bawdy*. Rev. ed. New York: Dutton.

Plutarch. [1579] 1964. *The life of Marcus Antonius*. Trans. T. North. In vol. 5 of *Narrative and dramatic sources of Shakespeare*, 254–318. *See* Bullough 1957–1973.

Quinn, E. 1985. Introd. to *The Shakespeare hour*, ed. Quinn, ix–xxv. New York: NAL.

Rabkin, N. 1967. *Shakespeare and the common understanding*. New York: Free.

Rackin, P. 1972. Shakespeare's boy Cleopatra, the decorum of nature, and the golden world of poetry. *PMLA* 87:201–12.

Ribner, I. 1959. "Then I denie you starres." In *Studies in the English Renaissance drama,*. ed. J. Bennett, O. Cargill, and V. Hall, Jr., 269–86. London: Owen.

Rich, A. 1978. Twenty-one love poems. In *The dream of a common language*. New York: Norton.

Riefer, M. 1984. "Instruments of some more mightier member." *Shakespeare Quarterly* 35:157–69.

Rose, M. B. 1988. *The expense of spirit*. Ithaca and London: Cornell University Press.

Rougemont, D. de [1940] 1983. *Love in the western world*. Trans. M. Belgion. Rev. ed. Princeton, N.J.: Princeton University Press.

Rubin, G. 1975. The traffic in women. In *Toward an anthropology of women*, ed. R. R. Reiter. New York: Monthly Review.

Rucker, M., Dir. 1989. *Romeo and Juliet*. Shakespeare/Santa Cruz.

Said, E. 1978. *Orientalism*. New York: Vintage.

Schücking, L. L. 1922. *Character problems in Shakespeare's plays*. London: Harrap.

Shakespeare, W. 1974. *The Riverside Shakespeare*. Ed. G. B. Evans. Boston: Houghton.

Shoaf, R. A. 1988. "For there is figures in everything." Paper read at General Session A. Sixth Citadel Conference on Literature, 10–12 March, Charleston, S.C.

Smith, M. 1966. *Dualities in Shakespeare*. Toronto: University of Toronto Press.

Snyder, S. 1985. That ends well? Afterword to *The Shakespeare hour*. Dir. M. Squerciati. Prod. H. Bellin and T. Kieffer. PBS-TV, WNET, New York.

Spurgeon, C. 1930. Leading motives in the imagery of Shakespeare's tragedies. Pub. of the Shakespeare Assn. 15:1–17.

———. 1935. *Shakespeare's imagery and what it tells us*. New York: Macmillan.

Stallybrass, P. 1989. Embodied politics. Abstract of paper presented at seminar, Materialist-Feminist Criticism of Shakespeare. Annual meeting of Shakespeare Assn. of America, 13–15 April, Austin.

Stallybrass, P., and A. White. 1986. *The politics and poetics of transgression*. London: Methuen.

Stanton, K. 1987. Male gender-crossing in *Othello*. Paper presented at seminar, Shakespearean Tragedy and Gender. Annual meeting of Shakespeare Assn. of America, 9–11 April, Seattle.

Stauffer, D. [1949] 1964. The school of love. In *Shakespeare*, ed. A. Harbage, 28–33. Englewood Cliffs, N.J.: Prentice. (First published in *Shakespeare's world of images*. New York: Norton.)

Stilling, R. 1976. *Love and death in Renaissance tragedy*. Baton Rouge: Louisiana State University Press.

Stirling, B. 1956. *Unity in Shakespearian tragedy*. New York: Columbia University Press.

Stoll, E. E. [1930] 1958. *Poets and playwrights*. Repr. Minneapolis: University of Minnesota Press.

Thomas, K. 1959. The double standard. *Journal of the History of Ideas*. 20:195–216.

Thompson, K. 1971. *Modesty and cunning*. Ann Arbor: University of Michigan Press.

Traversi, D. [1956] 1969. *An approach to Shakespeare.* 2 vols. 3rd rev. ed. New York: Doubleday.

Vickers, N. 1985. "The blazon of sweet beauty's best." In *Shakespeare and the question of theory. See* Parker and Hartman 1985, 95–115.

Whitaker, V. 1965. *The mirror up to nature.* San Marino: Huntington Library.

Wilson, H. 1957. *On the design of Shakespearian tragedy.* University of Toronto Dept. of English Studies and Texts, no. 5. Toronto: University of Toronto Press.

Wilson, J. D. [1950] 1973. Introd. to *Antony and Cleopatra,* ed. Wilson, vii–xxxvi. Repr. London: Cambridge University Press.

Woodbridge, L. 1987. Black and white and red all over. *Renaissance Quarterly* 40:247–97.

Zeffirelli, F., Dir. 1968. *Romeo and Juliet.* With L. Whiting and O. Hussey. BHE–London, Verona Productions, D. de Laurentiis.

Index

Page numbers of chapter-length discussions of specific protagonists and plays are indicated in boldface type.